The Hidden World of Autism

of related interest

The Complete Guide to Asperger's Syndrome
Tony Attwood
ISBN 978 1 84310 495 7

All Cats Have Asperger Syndrome
Kathy Hoopmann
ISBN 978 1 84310 481 0

Autistic Planet
Jennifer Elder
Marc Thomas and Jennifer Elder
ISBN 978 1 84310 842 9

Autism and Me
Rory Hoy
ISBN 978 1 84310 546 6

An Exact Mind
An Artist With Asperger Syndrome
Peter Myers, Simon Baron-Cohen and Sally Wheelwright
ISBN 978 1 84310 032 4

Brotherly Feelings
Me, My Emotions, and My Brother with Asperger's Syndrome
Sam Frender and Robin Schiffmiller
Illustrated by Dennis Dittrich
ISBN 978 1 84310 850 4

A Will of His Own
Reflections on Parenting a Child with Autism - Revised Edition
Kelly Harland
Foreword by Jane Asher, President of the National Autistic Society
ISBN 978 1 84310 869 6

Crystalline Lifetime
Fragments of Asperger Syndrome
Luke Jackson
ISBN 978 1 84310 443 8

Do You Understand Me?
My Life, My Thoughts, My Autism Spectrum Disorder
Sofie Koborg Brøsen
ISBN 978 1 84310 464 3

Parenting Across the Autism Spectrum
Unexpected Lessons We Have Learned
Maureen F. Morrell and Ann Palmer
ISBN 978 1 84310 807 8

The Hidden World of Autism

Writing and Art by Children
with High-functioning Autism

Rebecca Chilvers

Foreword by Uttom Chowdhury

Jessica Kingsley Publishers
London and Philadelphia

Photograph on page 32 reproduced with kind permission from Temple Grandin

First published in 2007
by Jessica Kingsley Publishers
116 Pentonville Road
London N1 9JB, UK
and
400 Market Street, Suite 400
Philadelphia, PA 19106, USA

www.jkp.com

Copyright © Rebecca Chilvers 2008
Foreword copyright © Uttom Chowdhury 2008

Library of Congress Cataloging in Publication Data
A CIP catalog record for this book is available from the Library of Congress

British Library Cataloguing in Publication Data
A CIP catalogue record for this book is available from the British Library

ISBN 978 184310 451 3

Printed and bound in the People's Republic of China

The Hidden World of Autism is dedicated to the families and children I have met through the Social Communication Disorders Clinic at Great Ormond Street Hospital. You are the inspiration and motivation behind this book.

Acknowledgements

I would like to thank a number of people who have supported the writing of this book: my colleagues at the Behavioural and Brain Sciences Unit for reading chapters and offering advice, the Ciao Bellas for red wine, laughter and special friendship, Pippa S. for all the hours you have listened, my parents, Pam and George, and brother Eddie for their enthusiasm and creativity, and Barry Flutter for your endless love, encouragement and patience.

Contents

Foreword

Despite the advances in medical research over the last fifty years, we are only just beginning to get a better understanding of the condition known as autism or autistic spectrum disorder. We hear endless debates about possible causes of the condition, numerous arguments over the criteria for making a diagnosis, and ongoing discussions on various treatment packages; the majority of which have no evidence base at all. While researchers and clinicians continue to attempt to understand the condition looking at genetics, brain images, and controlled treatment trials, one area of research that is neglected is the emotions, feelings and thoughts of the young person with autism. *The Hidden World of Autism* is a book that fills this neglected research area on the subject and helps the reader get a better understanding of the experience of young people with autism.

Rebecca Chilvers has managed to put together an amazing book that combines scientific research and theory with fascinating and poignant first person accounts of young people with autism. The brilliant drawings, stories and poems remind the reader that behind a diagnosis and label lies a young person who may be creative, intelligent, sad, interesting, funny, different, but above all, a young person who has feelings and thoughts and should be respected.

Professionals reading this book have a lot to learn about what it feels like to be autistic and will hopefully think more carefully about how they talk to young people and families about the subject of autism. Parents and siblings can learn a lot about how the condition affects family life and gain a better understanding of the family member with autism. Teachers who have a child with autism in their classroom should read Chapter 3, one of the best pieces of text ever written on school life for children with autism. The young person with autism will feel less isolated when reading about the experiences of other young people with the condition.

In summary, this is a truly wonderful book that covers all aspects of living with autism and the inner mind of the autistic child. There is a quote I remember from Harper Lee's *To Kill a Mockingbird* (1960): 'You never really understand a person until you consider things from his point of view…until you climb into his skin and walk in it'. This book allows you to 'climb into the skin' of someone with autism and get a viewpoint that is invaluable and fascinating, and at the same time give you an insight into the hidden world of autism.

Uttom Chowdhury,
Honorary Consultant in Child and Adolescent Psychiatry,
Social Communication Disorders Clinic,
Great Ormond Street Hospital, London.

Chapter 1

Introduction

The cause is hidden, but the effect is visible to all.

Ovid

Since about 1994, autism has changed from being a condition almost no one had heard of to being the subject of almost daily headlines. It has become a governmental issue, a public health issue and a matter of impassioned debate. To some, the increase in diagnosis represents an over-zealous medical profession eager to pathologise children who are in any way 'atypical'. To others, the battle to get their child recognised as autistic has been a long and painful process, met with criticism, blame and self-doubt. Every family has their own story about how their child came to be diagnosed with a social communication disorder, but so too have many children.

There are several different ways in which people come to a knowledge of what autistic children are like. Some encounter such children through textbooks or diagnostic manuals, which list a set of criteria that must be checked off as 'present' on a list. Others have seen films like *Rain Man*, and feel they have an accurate and encompassing grasp of what autism means. More recently, the media have suggested (on very little medical evidence) that some high-profile criminals have autism, which leads them to attack others or act antisocially.

Those who live with autistic individuals, however, know there is more to them than a list of 'symptoms', and that their complex and idiosyncratic natures cannot be reduced to features on a questionnaire or the summary of a clinician's brief interview. Many parents have written moving accounts of their children and family life, which illustrate these points with realism, emotion and humour, and there is no doubt that these accounts are hugely comforting and helpful to families living in similar circumstances. But is anyone listening to the children themselves, and when do they get a chance to speak?

Hundreds of clinics across the country are now equipped to assess children for autism, a process which relies heavily on parental interview and report. Until comparatively recently, diagnostic observations of children were not made and children often sat in a clinic without being spoken to. Some did not attend appointments at all. Although this is changing, it is very rare indeed for a child with autism to be asked their opinion or given a chance to express how they feel about the 'diagnosis' they have received and the impact it will have on their life. It is erroneously believed that they cannot have any understanding or insight into their condition, and therefore have nothing to tell us that we don't already know. Having met hundreds of children and young people with autistic spectrum disorders (including autism, Asperger Syndrome and Pervasive Developmental Disorder [PSD]), I have learnt that in discounting their personal experiences we may miss the most important questions (and maybe the answers) that science has sought to explain. This collection of writings and illustrations from children with autistic spectrum disorders aims to give them a voice in the hope that we learn to listen.

Notes for reading and using *The Hidden World of Autism*
What's in a name? Labelling social communication disorders

Autistic disorder applies to individuals who have social interaction impairments, communication impairments and repetitive, stereotypic and restricted interests and activities prior to 36 months of age. A number of criteria are set out in a DSM-1V *Diagnostic and Statistical Manual of Mental Disorders* (American Psychiatric Association 2000) used by professionals. There is another set of very similar criteria in the manual used by professionals in Europe called *The International Classification of Diseases*, Tenth Revision (ICD-10) (World Health Organisation 1993).

Despite the presence of these criteria, there is a great amount of confusion among professionals and lay people about the terms used to describe social communication disorders. Terms used vary between clinics, countries and individual clinicians and researchers. There are diagnostic manuals which outline the criteria for autism, Asperger Syndrome, atypical autism and Pervasive Developmental

Disorder – Not Otherwise Specified (PDD-NOS), although the criteria are not clear-cut enough to allow unambiguous interpretation.

There are many misconceptions and debates regarding the differences between autism and high-functioning autism, PDD-NOS and Asperger Syndrome, 'childhood autism' and atypical autism. Many parents much prefer the term Asperger Syndrome to autism, even when it is not strictly correct (to receive a diagnosis of Asperger Syndrome, it is essential that there is no language delay in infancy). Additionally, there are some occasions when clinicians might use a different term in a report to allow access to specific educational provision or state benefits.

In this book, for the sake of simplicity, 'autism' will be used as a term to cover all the terminology mentioned previously. There are still major debates about the differences (or lack of differences) between children who fit into each group, and covering these debates is not the purpose of this book. When terms other than autism or high-functioning autism are used, there is either an expressed reason for using these, or the children have used a different term themselves in their writing and their choice of terminology has not been changed.

Becoming a discerning reader of autism research

At the time of writing this book, typing 'autism' into the Google search engine generated 18,900,000 hits. There is no doubt about the explosion of writing and research on autism, not to mention institutions offering 'miracle cures', treatment programmes and seminars. How does the reader begin to discriminate good from poor research, and to evaluate new findings as they appear?

First, the most valuable and trustworthy research comes from scientific journals which operate a peer review system. This means that the articles have been reviewed by leading scientists in the field, and would not be published if the methodology or conclusions were thought to be scientifically suspect. Searching for research on websites such as PubMed or looking in the journals themselves should ensure a high quality of scientific work. Articles that are not peer reviewed, or are published online without critical appraisal, are likely to have serious flaws, which may make the results unreliable. One of the most common examples of this is the multitude of treatment trials for autism. When considering whether a treatment is effective, the trial needs to be 'double blind'. This means that neither the family/child receiving the treatment *nor* the professional administering it know which group they have been assigned to. For example, if a child is taking an experimental drug for treating aggressive behaviour and the parent knows whether they are receiving the actual drug or a placebo, it may alter their perception of the child's behaviour, independently of whether the treatment is having an effect or not. Equally, if the scientist knows which drug the child is taking, it may alter how they rate behaviour in the trial outcome. Many trials posted on the internet or in smaller non-peer reviewed publications are not double blind – therefore, the results are not conclusive or reliable indicators of treatment effectiveness.

Second, when reading any published research about autism, it is vital that one is aware of the variability covered by that term. Research involving children who are mute with severe learning disabilities is not going to be applicable to high-functioning children, and vice versa. When reading a research study, look carefully at who the participants are, and consider whether they are similar to your child. Are the children of similar intelligence? Have they had the same kind of treatment, or no treatment? Do they have special educational provision? Are they verbal? How old are they? There are many important variables which affect the outcome and generalisability of research studies. If your child is very different from the children in the study, the results are unlikely to be helpful to you. The majority of research is still with autistic children who have learning disabilities, despite these children being in the minority (figures given by the Medical Research Council state more than 70 per cent of children with autism have normal intelligence). It is therefore important to read studies such as outcome studies with a degree of caution, because they will almost certainly not be appropriate if a child has high-functioning autism or Asperger Syndrome. As a general guide, for children who have a diagnosis of high-functioning autism, literature on Asperger Syndrome is likely to be more pertinent than literature on autism.

Third, it is important to be aware of the nature and standards of the different methods used to diagnose children included in research. Some studies screen participants for autism using a full developmental, multi-agency assessment involving a team of highly qualified psychologists, speech and language therapists, and paediatricians. Others may use a tool as brief as a 12-item questionnaire to make the same diagnosis. It is clear that these two methods, and numerous variations in between, will result in groups of children who may be very different indeed. Therefore, if a particular outcome is hugely variable for two groups of children, both with autism and receiving the same treatment, the reason can often be found in how accurately they are assigned a diagnosis in the first place.

Finally, clinicians and researchers alike are not in agreement about how terms such as 'autism', 'PSD', 'Asperger Syndrome' and 'atypical autism' should be used. A child with the same set of behaviours could be assigned to a different category in a different study, depending on the diagnostic manual used (ICD-10 or DSM-IV), clinical opinion or subjective inclusion/exclusion criteria. This means that, if your child has Asperger Syndrome, it is not necessarily judicious to discard all research relating to high-functioning autism as many institutions do not make this distinction. Diagnostic issues such as these are likely to remain until more carefully considered criteria are developed in the future (see Chapter 1, p.12)

Using children's writing and pictures

The aim of this book is to give a voice to children with autism, while placing the issues they raise in a research and practice context. It is hoped that the children's contributions may offer a starting point for discussion about issues such as bullying, self-image, and the diagnosis of autism itself and what it means. The inclusion of pictures is also intended to stimulate non-verbal means of conveying ideas and feelings, which may be more appropriate for children who find verbal expression more challenging.

It is also hoped that parents, teachers and other professionals will find the content of this book useful in discussing these important issues with their children and patients, and that they themselves will find the contributions from the children stimulating, thought-provoking and challenging.

Notes about the children's contributions

The children's work has been reproduced exactly as it was originally worded. Correction of spelling is the only alteration made to some contributions. All original use of grammar is maintained as are unusual choices of words or phrases, which are seen as integral to accurately representing the children's thoughts and feelings.

Writing on illustrations has been transcribed when it is difficult to read, and interpretations and context have been provided by parents of younger children where necessary. All work is by the children themselves, and the themes of the book have been created around their choice of topics. The age of a child is recorded on their contribution as the age at which the work was completed; this may differ from their current age as given in their biography.

All the children have given their written consent to be included in this book.

Chapter 2

What's so Different about Me?
Life on the Autistic Spectrum

'Self-portrait' by Owen Oakley Darwin, aged 10

'My world called autism' by Janet Weedon-Skinner, aged 17

I have a confession
About my obsession
From the clean to the depraved
There's no cure for my depression,
Which fuels my obsessions.
Dim the lights,
It burns my eyes.
Don't make a sound,
It bursts my ear drums.
Don't touch me,
It makes my skin bleed.
Don't think I am so shy,
Once you get to know me,
You'd think I was normal.
Don't cry that I can't look into your eyes.
I can still look at your nose.
Don't think I'm dumb
If your words seem foreign.
Don't laugh at me if I fall or spill.
I'm only human
I'm like you.
I just think different.
Don't look at me like I'm a child.
Your words may seem foreign
But I'm smarter than you think.
So don't cry for me.
I am what I am.
I'm special, just like you.

Janet's poem makes a poignant and bold statement about having autism. She acknowledges that there are aspects of life she experiences differently and things she does differently. However, at the same time, there are many things about her that make her the same as any young women of her age. It asks the question 'What is so different?' and how can we understand what those differences are. Reflecting on their childhood, many adults with autism, some who received a formal diagnosis later on in life, describe vividly how they had always felt different from other people. Some recall not understanding 'unwritten' rules when interacting with others, or being confused that they couldn't make or maintain friendships despite frequently trying. This chapter is a collection of writings and illustrations from children about what it's really like to have autism and to know about it earlier on in life. The first piece of writing is by Jordao, who addresses the issue of whether he feels different or 'normal' in his life, and whether being autistic is something he wants other people to know about. The second piece of writing is by Jake, who discusses some of the difficulties he has in relating to others, and the aspects of life that can cause him anxiety. He also describes things in his life that make him happy.

Extract from 'About me' by Jordao Allen, aged 15

My name is Jordao Allen. I am autistic. Before I was diagnosed, I felt a bit confused to understand about myself. I thought to myself so if I'm autistic, am I still a bit normal or do I feel like a freak like the other disables? Ah man! Now I'll have to go to the Paralympics in London I think. I now feel a bit normal and deep inside I feel I want to do something stupid, but I don't want to because I want to get on with my life and get with my work. So I don't feel autism is really a bad thing, but sometimes you need to keep it a secret.

I'm from the Caribbean (Well actually my family came from the Caribbean so I'm British Caribbean). I was born in St George's hospital in Tooting in Wandsworth, London. I have three brothers and a sister. When I was young, my parents split up. It was a very bad turn of events but it was a very easy thing to accept. Our brotherhood is threatened to be splitting up too. Two of my brothers live with mama, and my little brother and I lives with my dad and been raised differently. My hobbies are eating, drinking, play football, PS2 and shopping in popular places like Piccadilly.

My favourite things of my hobbies are eating Chinese food, supporting and playing like Man. United, drinking tropical juice and playing the PS2 (and soon PSP and mostly PS3).

Apart from autism, there's nothing unusual about me.

Extract from 'Me, myself and my disorders' by Jake Ballard, aged 17

My name is Jake Michael Lavous Ballard. I was born on Tuesday 6th of June 1989 at Frimley Park Hospital at 10.55 p.m. I have Asperger Syndrome, Obsessive Compulsive Disorder and Bipolar Disorder, which is often called manic depression. I was diagnosed with Asperger Syndrome when I was 9 years old however I wasn't told until I was 10 years old. I will describe some things about Asperger Syndrome. For instance when I am nervous I fiddle with my ear and I can't always make eye contact with people. I can make eye contact with my mum and dad, other family members and my best friend Craig, but it's not something I find easy.

Also the way I am fussy about food in a certain order. Also I am sensitive to really strong flavours. I sometimes find it hard to understand people's conversation and also their point of view. I can get easily confused by instructions. I like things kept simple and I like to have a routine. Here are a few things I find disturbing:

Fire alarms, loud noises such as fireworks, strong smells, being shut in somewhere, darkness (I was terrified during the 1999 eclipse), the thought of travelling on an aeroplane (I WILL NEVER GO ON AN AEROPLANE), breaking my routines, other people breaking the rules, being in the house without my mum or dad, uncomfortable clothes. The sight of sloppy foods like porridge or mashed up Weetabix (it is making me feel sick now just thinking about it), touching the bin. These are just a few. I could go on forever (not literally).

Here are a few things I really like:

Pot Noodles, cocktail sausages, sausage rolls (I have routines and rituals regarding these when I eat), music (especially Parklife and Bohemian Rhapsody), Eastenders, making lists, car valeting, time and timing things, swimming, spending time with Craig, going in the hydro pool, walking and bike riding with my mum and dad (especially if I go through the traffic lights!), word searches, being a passenger in the car, playing a football game being Liverpool on the computer (to make my mum proud as she is Liverpool mad), washing up (according to my rituals), collecting 1ps, 2ps and 5ps, spotting and counting Citroen cars when I'm out (my favourite car is a green Citroen Picasso), boiling the kettle to make tea, coffee and hot drinks.

In Chapter 5 we will hear more about some of the obsessions and rituals Jake has, how he understands them and how he lives with them.

Comorbidity in autism

Autistic spectrum disorders often occur with other psychiatric or neurodevelopmental disorders, most commonly Attention Deficit Hyperactivity Disorder (ADHD) (40–50% depending on age of assessment Gadow *et al.* 2005), anxiety (35% Gadow *et al.* 2005) and depression (30% Wing 1981, 37% Ghaziuddin, Weidmer-Mikhail and Ghaziuddin 1998). These rates are significantly higher than those found in the general population. A study by Ghaziuddin *et al.* (1998) found that 65 per cent of adolescents classified in the study as having Asperger Syndrome presented with symptoms of an additional psychiatric disorder at the time of evaluation or at a two-year follow up.

Studies on comorbidity in autism are few because conditions such as ADHD are specified *not* to be diagnosed in addition to autism in some diagnostic manuals, and therefore these comorbid conditions have received little attention or treatment. More recently, clinicians are including assessment of psychiatric and other neurodevelopmental disorders such as ADHD in an autism assessment, because the presence of these additional symptoms has implications for effective treatment (such as adapting cognitive behavioural therapy [CBT] to tailor it to the needs of children with autism [White 2004], outcome in adulthood and access to services).

When making the diagnosis of a separate condition, it is sometimes difficult to ascertain which symptoms may be categorised separately to autism and which might be a manifestation of some autistic traits. For example, obsessions can be part of autism and obsessive-compulsive disorder (OCD), so how and when is the distinction made and a separate condition added? This is an important question because, if an additional condition such as OCD is not treated and intervention is only given for autism, a child could become progressively worse, with the erroneous conclusion that it is their autism that is causing the disintegration of functioning. Additionally, it is possible that children and young people with autism may manifest symptoms of anxiety or depression differently from typically developing children (Kim *et al.* 2000). There is already some work by Leyfer *et al.* (2006) examining how psychiatric disorders can be reliably assessed when autism is already present. Further research is needed to examine all these issues. For further reading examining comorbidity and autism in detail, see Ghaziuddin (2006). In the following extract, Jake describes what it is like to have Asperger Syndrome and Bipolar Disorder as well as autism.

Extract from 'Me, myself and my disorders' by Jake Ballard, aged 17

The other condition I have is Bipolar Disorder or manic depression. Since I have had help from Great Ormond Street Hospital this has not been as much of a problem because I now take medication to help control my mood. In the past when I was low I felt that I didn't want to do anything. I used to be sick a lot and feel sad, tired and weak and ill. When I was really bad I just wanted to sit and rest with my mum and didn't like it if she wasn't near me. I had to have help to do everything. When I got really high I felt like I was in charge of the whole world like I WAS GOD or something.

I behaved like a maniac and made a fool out of myself a lot of the time. It makes me sad thinking about being very high or very low because I feel quite balanced and feeling the way I used to is not nice to think about. It brings back bad memories which I feel are in my past. I have accepted some things about myself; the fact that I may not be able to drink much alcohol because of my medication, the fact I won't be able to drive as there is too much to have to concentrate on at one time and I am easily distracted. I also think that I will always need a bit of help to get on in the world. To finish I will describe how I see myself. I see myself as a very obsessive person. I am a kind gent and I try and look out for people. I am very happy to have found a best friend at college. And I am DETERMINED to go through an amber light on my bike one day without causing an accident.

As we have seen, although these young people have been diagnosed with autism or Asperger Syndrome, each experiences it in a different way, with different aspects being more or less important in their lives. They also show a remarkable insight into their condition, an ability which has previously been thought to be missing or severely impaired in autistic people.

The artwork and piece of writing on pages 24 and 25 is by Owen. It was found by his mother and, when she asked what it was about, he explained that the 'Black Face' is his Asperger Syndrome. At the end of the story a ball of light hits his black face and it goes, and Owen isn't autistic anymore.

The following piece of writing by Connor raises another important issue, particularly when children may wish to explain to their peers what it means to have autism. Autism is a strange term to children, particularly those who are young, and they can have as many misconceptions about it as adults do. We learn from Connor that when one of his classmates heard the term 'Asperger Syndrome' they thought it was a bad disease, and how a simple explanation from a teacher resolved the misunderstanding.

'Being Asperger's' by Connor Smith, aged 10

I find it a lot harder to concentrate without something to fiddle with. The things I like to fiddle with are elastic bands, squidgies, and pencils and pens. I sometimes find it hard when teachers don't treat me very well. I get really angry. I like St Mary's Island school because it has nice plants. My old school had dead plants. At this school we have a nice playground and hardly any fights.

At my old school I was scared in Year 2 because my teacher would yell at me for accidentally dropping my book or pencil. Once I dropped my workbook down the side of the radiator and she wouldn't let me get it and she started complaining that I'd lost my book and it was actually her fault for not letting me get it. Really she should have complained about herself. Whenever I did something wrong it was the Asperger's but she would just think I was being naughty and stupid and tell me off. Whenever I went to the therapist she would say I don't care what the silly doctors say. You're normal and you shouldn't be going there.

I hate it when it's really hot. I feel ill and I can't concentrate on anything. When my teacher said something about Asperger's one of my friends thought it was a bad disease. Mrs Smith said that it's not a disease, and it is something that some people are born with. Mrs Smith explained it well and the class knew what it was.

I sometimes get upset and say I'm not human. I don't have very high confidence with myself in art and P.E. I was chosen to represent the school at cross-country running but I dropped out after the race started.

The good things about Asperger's makes you better at some things that other children aren't as good as, like quiz programmes, like Vorderman's Big Brain Game. It has really stupid questions that people should be able to answer really quickly but sometimes they get them wrong. It's the adults that answer them. I'm not too good at remembering some things, like maths as in times tables.

'Black face' by Owen Oakley Darwin, aged 10

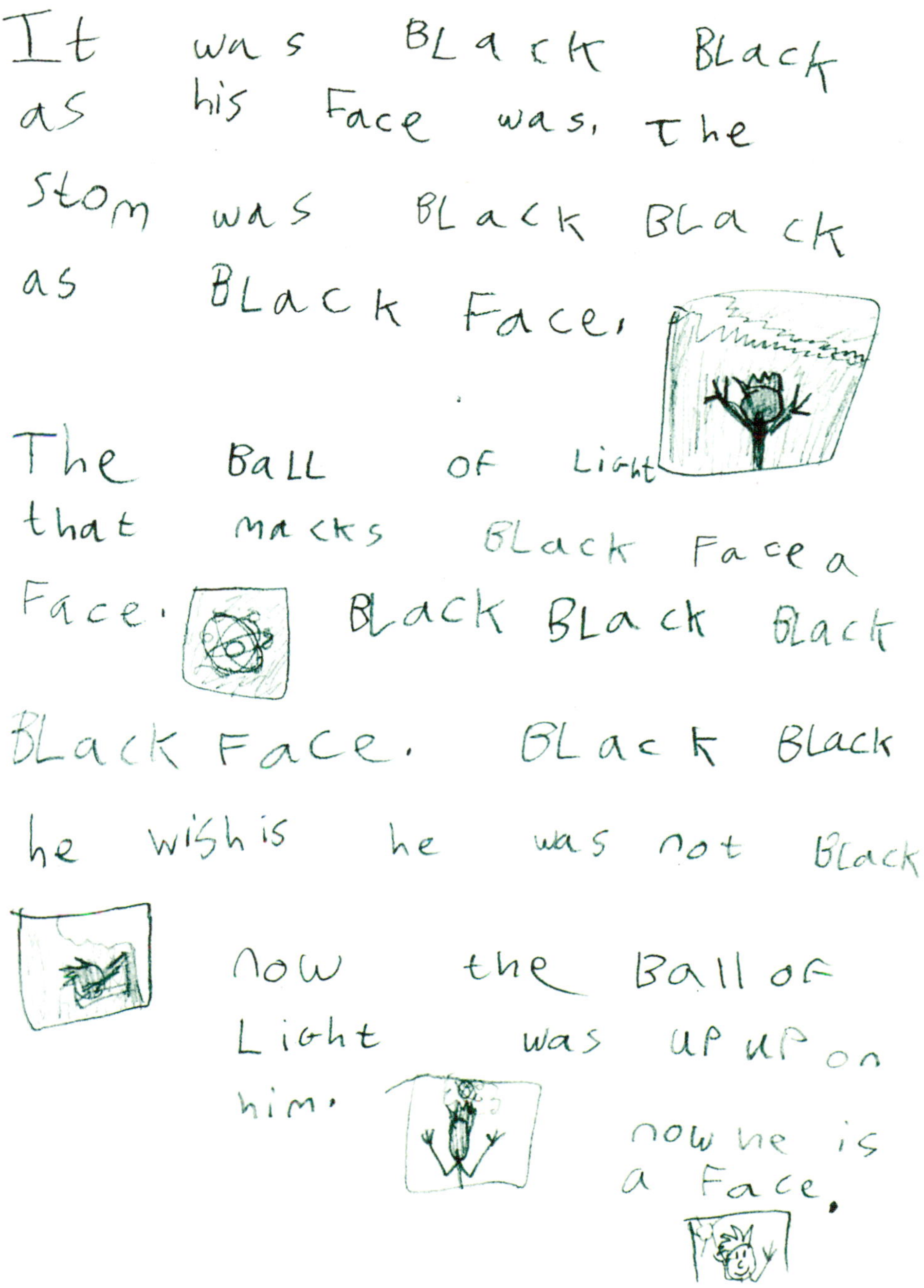

It was BLack Black
as his Face was, The
stom was BLack BLack
as BLack Face,

The BaLL of Light
that macks Black Face a
Face. BLack BLack Black

BLack Face. BLack Black

he wishis he was not Black

now the BaLl of
Light was up up on
him, now he is
a Face,

'It was Black Black as his face was. The storm was Black Black as Black Face. The ball of light that makes Black Face a face. Black Black Black Black face. Black Face wishes he was not black. Now the ball of light was up up on him. Now he is a face.'

Nathan also describes how he worried when he first received a diagnosis of autism spectrum disorder (ASD), because he thought it was a disease. It is understandable how this idea may emerge, as many children have to go for an assessment to a clinic in a hospital where there are a lot of children who are very poorly. However, finding out more about Asperger Syndrome changed his views on what it meant for himself and those around him.

'When I found out I had an ASD' by Nathan Cash Davidson, aged 18

When I found out I had an ASD I was worried because I related disability to people in wheel chairs. I thought it was a disease.

At first I thought it was rare but then I found out that loads of other people had similar things.

I think people should be jealous of having Asperger's because you can overcome lots of aspects of it and then you are left with the talent, in my case, I can beatbox, rap, paint; play the guitar, and I have a really good imagination. I can invent marble runs and sculpt if I want to, which is almost like a robot and people should be jealous. Check out my painting in the book bruv (Chapter 6, pp.97–102).

I think I need Asperger's to fit into the community of people who have similar things like ADHD or ASD So the people who don't are the odd ones out.

When I was at school it was fairly hard to make new friends I had one friend who I spent a lot of time with he had Asperger's as well. The teachers at school sometimes had a problem with me. I don't think most of the teachers understood Asperger's. I was told off for giggling which used to happen quite frequently. I often giggle in stressful situations.

At my sixth form college it was easier to socialise with people where they weren't always fighting like at school. I used to talk to a group of girls who were "buff."

Michelangelo had Asperger's too, and he was a great master. I think my ideas are original and have a different angle to them.

I did get picked on at school, but mostly in the first few years. Later as they got older people calmed down and I had less problems. By year 10, 11 everything was fine. In year 7 and 8 I had constant threats there were 3 people who beat me up. Sometimes I was pushed into chairs and someone punched me and poked me with scissors. There was one boy who did most of the bullying I wasn't the only one that got the attention. Most of the other people in my class got bullied at some point.

My secondary school was reopened after years of being closed; I used to go to a weekend music school there before it went back to being a high school. I learned the French horn. Then one day I found myself in the same room which was a science Lab but I thought it was strange that now Kids were fighting in there instead of playing music.

Perspectives through poetry

Patrick and Ryan have chosen poems to express their thoughts about themselves in two very different styles – Patrick describes how he sees himself and what he enjoys doing, and Ryan uses an acrostic to explain what having autism means to him, followed by an illustration of himself walking his dog, Brock.

'What it's like to be Patrick' by Patrick Harper, aged 9

Patrick is tall,
Patrick is bold,
Patrick is nice,
Patrick likes gold.

Patrick is happy,
Patrick likes competitions,
Patrick is lovely,
Patrick always listens.

Patrick likes recording,
Patrick likes computers,
Patrick likes his XDA but...most of all...
MOST OF ALL!..........

Patrick loves Mum!

'Ryan's autism' by Ryan Boatright, aged 13

Autism makes me angry
Understanding is not easy
To read my books in peace is such a treat
I love to be tidy and neat
Sleep is hard to get
My gardening always calms me down

'Me walking my dog, Brock' by Ryan Boatright, aged 13

Telling children about their diagnosis

One of the most common questions parents ask in clinics is when should they tell their child they have autism or Asperger Syndrome. Some feel that having an explanation for the way their son or daughter experiences life may be beneficial to them. For example, many children with social communication difficulties find it hard to make friends, but may blame themselves or become very confused about why they can't seem to do something all their peers can. At other times, parents feel they don't wish their child to feel different in any way, and that by having a 'label', they may feel there is something fundamentally 'wrong' with them. As children get older, they may also feel that the diagnosis is not fair or accurate, and this can cause resentment towards their parents and professionals who have been involved. The following two pieces examine both sides of this issue – Brendan who feels there has been a definite set of negative consequences since his diagnosis, and Martin who views his diagnosis as 'lifting a veil of confusion'.

'How autism has changed my life' by Brendan Young, aged 16

Life before being diagnosed was no different to me than it was after. Autism totally ruined my teenage life thanks to council/government and/or social service's regulations and rules that I or my friends/mates can't go off and socialise by ourselves without an adult until I'm at least 16, meaning I have to put up with hours and hours of having to wait for my parent(s) leaving me indoors in front of the T.V. when I could and want be playing football, arcade games and other fun activities like all other teenagers.

'Life before being diagnosed' and 'What's so different about me?' by Martin Hal-fead, aged 14

LIFE BEFORE BEING DIAGNOSED

Life before I was diagnosed was, apparently, an extremely confusing time for those around me, especially my close family. My mum had only occasionally noticed that my behaviour stuck out like a sore thumb. Often this behaviour was patchy, fleeting, and was only really noticeable when closely compared to other children's behaviour. All of this conspired to prevent me from being diagnosed for years. When I was finally diagnosed with Asperger Syndrome, it was a gust of wind, lifting once and for all the veil of confusion that had hung over me for several years.

WHAT'S SO DIFFERENT ABOUT ME?

I think that Asperger Syndrome doesn't make me feel that different from other people. Overall it makes very little impact on my perception of life. Asperger Syndrome isn't for me a major issue in my life because I believe that people around me do not often see my behaviour as different to theirs and therefore Asperger Syndrome has never taken a sentient form in my life. I personally am aware of it occasionally but it generally tends to sink to the bottom of my mind, only to be dredged up when I need to become aware of it again.

Summary

Autism is a confusing diagnosis for children, even more so because so much confusion still exists among the professionals who make the diagnoses. It is also a difficult diagnosis for those around the child to accept and understand, and it may come as a surprise, a disaster or a relief to families and schools.

The children who have written about what autism means to them in this chapter illustrate the variation in experience. While some see being diagnosed as wholly negative, others feel it has enabled them to understand something fundamental about themselves, which isn't 'abnormal' or 'odd' but different. With increasing knowledge and understanding, it is hoped more people will accept that, rather than being a categorically separate condition removed from 'normal' experience, autism is at the extreme of a continuum of behaviours seen in us all.

Chapter 3

School

I couldn't stand it seeing him so distressed. It was a last resort but I had to take him out of school and educate him at home...it's exhausting.

Parent of 12-year-old autistic boy

She was known as a loner, a drifter; continuously bullied and ostracised at school.

Parent of 16-year-old autistic girl

Many people consider their school-days as one of the happiest times in their lives – a time when there were no pressures and stresses, a time to learn new things and have new experiences, and maybe to make life-long friendships. Unfortunately this is not everyone's experience of school, and for young people with autism many will find it a challenging and upsetting experience, which will affect them long into adulthood.

Autism is no longer a rare condition teachers may come across once every few years. An average mainstream primary school is statistically likely to have five to six autistic children, and the average secondary school eight to ten, based on a prevalence rate of 1 per cent (Baird *et al.* 2006). In actuality, this may be a conservative figure. A report carried out by the National Autistic Society in 2000 (Barnard, Prior and Potter 2000) reported that the teachers surveyed felt that 1 in 86 children they taught had special needs related to an ASD. The implications of such figures cannot be under-estimated. They indicate that attention needs to be focused on how to make the experience of school easier for autistic children, and towards fostering an understanding of how to interpret behaviour.

Behavioural problems in the classroom and their link to social communication difficulties

Because of a poor understanding of social rules in a classroom, or the inability to follow a series of instructions, to name but a few, autistic children are often regarded as rude or 'trouble makers' in school. For example, they may insist on finishing a task while the rest of the class has moved on to another activity, or fail to understand that when a teacher raises their voice they are angry. Use of more abstract language in the classroom can also prove difficult to interpret and leads to frequent misunderstandings. For example, one autistic boy was told by his teacher to draw the curtains in the classroom. He sat down with a pen and paper and did just that. This caused him to be sent out of the class, and he was very confused about what he had done wrong. Being confused or distressed by a situation at school can cause children to lash out at others or shout at people in authority, leading to disciplinary action by the school. Another survey (Barnard *et al.* 2000) found that 21 per cent of autistic children had been excluded at some time in their education, and 17 per cent more than six times. The feelings of rejection and mis-understanding that can arise from these events often have a lasting impact on chil-dren's self-esteem and confidence. Adults with autism looking back on their school-days frequently report that no-one made an attempt to understand them, and that they felt unwanted by their schools.

Interestingly, the same conclusions can be drawn if the issue is looked at the other way round. Gilmour *et al.* (2004) examined a group of children who had been excluded, or were at high risk of exclusion from school, and found that over two-thirds of these children had social communication deficits comparable to autism. It was also found that many children who had a primary diagnosis of conduct disorder had unidentified social communication difficulties. These findings have major implications for how children are managed in school and the treatment they receive as part of their care. If in some cases social communication difficulties are at the root of behaviours that put children at risk of exclusion, then closely targeted intervention and acknowledgement may dramatically improve outcome for these children.

Educational attainment

High-functioning autistic children by definition have intelligence that falls in the normal range. Some children have exceptional abilities, as measured by formal IQ tests. Despite this, when teachers are asked to provide an estimate of a child's intelligence, it is often lower than that found at test. In some cases, the discrepancy is such that a child with an IQ in the 'very high' range is being educated in a moderate learning disabilities special school. What can account for these differences? First, the classroom environment itself may make it difficult for a child with autism to learn. If they find loud noise, unstructured time or social language difficult to deal with, learning is unlikely to take place. Often something as simple as having a timetable of the day on their desk to show what is happening next can allay some anxiety. Having a quiet place to go is also helpful and easily arranged in most school buildings. Second, it may be the case that a child with autism learns in a different way from their peers. Visual aids are commonly used, such as daily time-tables, pictures and graphs, to illustrate concepts and help children understand the structure of the school day (Moyes 2001). Also, autistic children are often interested in different aspects of learning material, such as facts, figures, technical processes and mechanisms. These interests can stand them in good stead for further education where a more limited area of focus is beneficial (such as writing computer programs or engineering a product), but they are not compatible with the broad curriculum taught in schools. Often having time outside school where specific interests can be encouraged and developed helps children to feel people are interested in what they value, and can act as an incentive to focus on school subjects in school hours as best they can.

Temple Grandin, a famous professor of animal science at Colorado State University who has autism, has had much to say about autistic individuals in the education system, particularly in regard to nurturing their often exceptional talents.

Professor Grandin came from a family of engineers and mathematicians and went on to design revolutionary equipment and guidelines for the humane treatment of livestock. In her school-days, she would certainly have been regarded as 'gifted', but she reports that many children with specific talents are not allowed to develop them at school because they do not have the social skills or they have an autism label (Grandin 2001). She also highlights that some 'autistic thinking' can be extremely beneficial, not only as the basis for technical achievement but also in the creative field. An autistic individual is often able to focus on aspects of a subject

Temple Grandin

for far longer than their 'neuro-typical' contemporaries. This is likely to pay off in further study where an in-depth understanding and an ability to concentrate for extended periods of time are essential, but something that people often find difficult to achieve. As the children's contributions to this book illustrate, the scope for imaginative ideas and perspectives is not absent from all autistic individuals and can help to create highly original and powerful work.

Fitting in at school

Perhaps the most distressing side of being at school for autistic children and those who care for them is the social difficulties they face. Children form social groups from a young age and, as they get older, understanding how these operate becomes increasingly complex. 'Getting in with the crowd' requires a good awareness of how the crowd functions – who the group leaders are, how they talk, how they dress, what music they listen to and so on. After assimilating this information, it is necessary to model your behaviour to fit in and be adaptable to changes when they occur, as well as picking up on the subtle group dynamics. This is a sizeable challenge to any young person with autism, requiring sophisticated social skill. It is therefore not surprising that many autistic children find themselves marginalised by other children who are all too ready to pick out differences (see also Chapter 4).

The following extract illuminates how it feels for a child to have Asperger Syndrome in secondary school.

Extract from 'The wrong side of the two-way mirror' by Louise Parker, aged 12

The title for this came because being aspie in school is like being on the reflective side of a two-way mirror. It feels this way because in a sense, the other kids can see you, but you can't see them. Another metaphor for this feeling would be to say that you are on Big Brother, but are the only housemate.

It all stems from aspie's inability to pick up social cues and convention, and therefore it can feel like the other kids are mind-readers in comparison to you, and believe me, they take advantage the best they can. Doing things that they know will confuse you, or things they know you will have no scripted response to. People will sometimes call out my name after me, sometimes in a deep voice, but mostly it's 'Hi Louise!' in a high, patronising tone. They know I won't respond. Maybe that is why they do it, maybe they said hello and meant it at first, but I took it as an insult, and ignored them. Now it's all a joke on their part, I do not answer.

At the moment I'm really quiet in my teaching group. I haven't made friends with anybody, and I don't usually speak unless I'm answering a question or if someone speaks to me. In late year five, after having been socially confident and almost inconspicuous for most of years four and five, I became like I am now. A bit of a loner, and quiet. This carried on into most of year six, but near the end I yet again strived to be 'normal'. Now in year seven, I am aspie again. Only this time I'm not desperate to be neurotypical.

I got my official Asperger's Syndrome diagnosis last year, and it has made everything easier to understand. Why I tell stories to myself out loud, why I don't know how to make friends, even why I bob as I walk (I wasn't actually aware I did this until a few weeks ago, when some people commented, then started mimicking me). I think that was a bit exaggerated as they were not so much walking as skipping, and I'm pretty sure I don't skip.

There are very few sane people in secondary school. Some are, and I don't mind talking to them, but most seem to lose all humanity when they move up to year seven. They become more immature, they begin this raging homophobia, and this incessant need to bully. Rather than saying 's'cuse' – or something like that – or just trying to edge through the gap, or go round you, they always shout 'Move!' or 'Get out of the way' when they want to get past. And they will pick on you, whether it's because they genuinely don't like you, or because you're year seven or your tie's too long, or simply because you're there and they felt like saying something stupid. I often feel like I'm sharing a class with hyperactive baboons, but much, much bitchier.

Louise's experience is sadly similar to that of many young people with autism, and emphasises the particular difficulty many children find in moving from primary to secondary school. Primary schools are smaller, and most still have just one or two teachers per year for the class. Secondary schools can be overwhelming when suddenly there are ten or more teachers to get used to, lessons in different classrooms, rotating timetables and older, less sympathetic pupils. The transition from primary to secondary school often instigates a referral for a diagnosis for those who have got by in a primary setting, and frequently causes anxiety or low mood in children who feel they no longer have the security of their previous school. In addition, special needs provision for children is often cut at the secondary level, leaving many autistic children with little or no help when they need it most. Interestingly, the rate of autistic spectrum disorders reported by teachers (Barnard *et al.* 2001) is three times higher in primary schools than secondary schools. This suggests that there are many undiagnosed children in the secondary system, but also that the diagnosis may be 'lost' or relabelled as a child passes into secondary education. Indeed, by the time a young person reaches adulthood, their chances of obtaining a diagnosis of autism are greatly reduced (as a result of current lack of awareness of social communication disorders in adult psychiatry and the unavailability of developmental histories) although there are likely to be just as many autistic individuals at every age.

The difficulty in adjusting to secondary school is amplified by the real increase in bullying in secondary education. Approximately 90 per cent of children who have attended the social communication disorders clinic at Great Ormond Street Hospital have experienced some form of bullying, be it physical, verbal or even sexual assault. In some cases, this has led to school refusal and self-harm. Due to difficulties in expressing thoughts and experiences, it may be hard for autistic children to tell others about bullying, and left unchecked it may go on for a number of years. The following pieces are written by Brendan Young, aged 16 and Jordao Allen, also 15 years old, who discuss the issue of bullying.

'My time at school' by Brendan Young, aged 16

I was bullied quite a bit at school, and thought the teachers were VERY slow, ignorant, lazy, uncaring, pitiful, incompetent etc and boy I can go on for ages in/with describing how badly they did in sorting out bullies. I only held back in having a fight because of my dad's career success and because of a certain girl I admired for a long period of time.

Extract from 'About me' by Jordao Allen, aged 15

I'm happy that I'm part of this school as the school is part of me. Some of the teaching assistants and teachers understands me.

I feel nothing when it comes to bullying, nothing at all. I was teased and bullied at school but not outside. I sometimes tease people and it make me feel ashamed. On my opinion, the teachers never do anything about it. The reasons why I'm tired some of the times at school is because I was doing the chores at home, working hard at school. I need freedom and go to bed late. Some people don't understand how I feel, especially by their looks and how they act.

I feel upset when I lose my good marks of the things I was good at – getting shouted at, my faults and receiving bad news slip for no good reasons because I don't want to ruin – how should I put it? – 'Family's pride'.

Brendan's anger at how he was treated at school and Jordao's shared sentiment that teachers did little to help highlights some of the issues that may arise in a bullying situation. Sometimes it is difficult for children to express their feelings of anger and injustice at how they have been treated, particularly if they feel they won't be believed or be able to communicate what has happened effectively. It is not uncommon for parents to find children coming home from school being aggressive and unco-operative with them, as a result of bad experiences during the day. One parent of an autistic child aged six reported, 'If he has had a bad day at school he can't express his feelings. He just trashes his room. He doesn't recognise his own feelings.'

Help with social relationships at school

Difficulties making and maintaining friendships are a hallmark of autistic spectrum disorders, and last long after school has finished. There are, however, schemes that help autistic children to interact more successfully with other children, and aim to foster a better understanding of their difficulties by others in their class. The most well-known scheme is 'Circle of Friends' (Newton, Taylor and Wilson 1996, Taylor 1997), which has also been shown not only to benefit the child with autism but also the other members of the school who take part (Whitaker *et al.* 1998). Autistic children also report that having a special skill, such as being good at computer games or knowing the story-line of a Harry Potter novel exceptionally well, can be a good starting point to strike up a friendship in the play-ground. Lunchtime clubs for chess or cards can also be a good place to meet other children with a common interest, and can help the sometimes awkward stage at the beginning of an interaction when it may be difficult to think of something to talk about. For more on friendships, see Chapter 4, p.64.

Support in school

Currently, there are many more autistic children in school than those catered for by statements of special educational need. Teachers and schools are under huge strain to provide extra help and resources to children with special needs, often with little or no extra funding. The Children's Commissioner for England, Professor Sir Al Aynsley-Green, commented recently: 'It's appalling and it's shameful for our country, the fifth richest economy in the world, to have so many children that are not being looked after and given the resources they need to develop their full potential' (2006). Despite this, many teachers make extra allowances on an unfunded basis to help autistic children, as experienced by Martin Hal-fead:

'School' by Martin Hal-fead, aged 14

I am very happy at school. My teachers understand my condition and do their level best to support throughout each school day. I don't think that schools should do more to help because there is a limit to how far a school can reasonably help a child out.

If a child is lucky enough to have some additional support in school, even for a few hours a week, this can have hugely beneficial effects if properly targeted. However, it can be difficult to get when an autistic child has intelligence in the normal range, and the process is not reported to be easy by parents. Despite this, it is certainly worth the effort as illustrated by Owen aged 10. Owen's mother comments that having help at school has 'helped him to feel good about himself…the difference Mrs Harvey has made to Owen is incredible'.

'My teachers' by Owen Oakley Darwin, aged 10

eVel sins She came my Life has Got Beer

I Mrs Havy

I have a HePr and shes called Mrs Hav,

She Plavs whiv Me.

'Mrs Harvey' by Owen Oakley Darwin, aged 10
'I have a helper and she's called Mrs Harvey. Ever since she came my life has got better. She plays with me.'

Starting a new school: A recollection and a story

Starting a new school can often be a particularly daunting experience for a child with autism, and it also causes parents a great deal of anxiety. Louise has written about life at secondary school earlier in this chapter, yet she still has vivid memories of how she felt during her early days at primary school. She recounts that first day again in the following extract in which the challenges of fitting into and interpreting a new school environment are described. Connor has written about what it's like to have Asperger Syndrome, and some of the issues he faced as he grew older in school in Chapter 2 (p.23). 'James' New School' (pp.43–52) is an account he wrote when he was starting primary school aged five about a boy like him called James. It illustrates by text, but also expressive pictures, the worries he had when he went to his new class and the difference it made when his teacher helped him find another boy to befriend him.

'At school: The earlier years' by Louise Parker, aged 12

I remember my first morning at school. That was all it was. A morning. We stayed only 'til lunchtime on our first day in Reception, or year 'R' at Fair Oak Infants in Eastleigh. I remember having to sit down, legs crossed, and Miss (Linda) Griffiths reading out the register. The class was one third its eventual size as the Autumn/Winter, Spring and Summer birthdays were staggered. By the end of the year I would learn the full register off by heart.

So us Autumn and Winter children had to sit down. Legs crossed, answer our names on the register then go off and do as we pleased. The others played with each other, I went off alone. There were these blue drawers with different coloured buttons and strings and things in them. I made a beach with the blue and yellow tiddlywinks counters and buttons. I was alone at break time too. I ran around, telling stories out loud to myself. No body seemed to notice.

Once we got to have lunch in the hall with the older children we soon found we could not eat the Mars Bar first. The dinner ladies would patrol round the packed lunch tables telling us it was sandwiches first. What I now know it meant was that we had to have our chocolate or cake last. Of course, I thought they really did mean we would be told off if we ate anything at all before our sandwiches so I made sure my sarnies were the first thing I had. I got into trouble with the head dinner lady for banging the rope on the gym climbing frame that was up against the wall. I think I was annoyed. Nobody told me. Or upset. Why did she shout?

I had a penchant for doing it Louise's way. I would tell stories at break time and if another child wanted to play with me (minus the two I wanted to be friends with – and could be tyrannical in ensuring that they played with me) then I would push them and shout at them. It was one girl (who strangely I would later befriend) who persisted. I got sent to the Headmistress for hitting this girl when she kept trying to sit next to me. Unfortunately, it didn't deter me from aggressive behaviour and I carried on into year one.

In year two the Louise Parker Way Or No Way At All attitude was still firmly in place, despite the fact that I now had better social skills and a couple of friends. I would run out of the room at random moments to read a book in the corridor. I got told off at first but then they let me. I was surprised when I got away with it. They must have known I was Aspie, or at least socially awkward long before they let on. I also refused to accept help, which is a trait I still have. I am an independent worker and strictly no help unless I want it.

James' New School

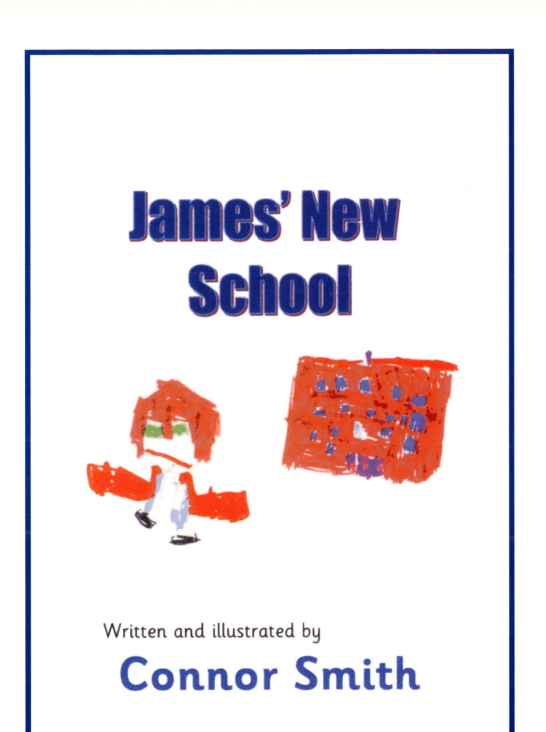

Written and illustrated by

Connor Smith

James was scared
when he went to a
new school.

His mum took
him in the car.

James met Mrs Mandy. She was going to be his teacher.

James went into the classroom

All the children sat on the carpet. James was sad because he didn't have any friends.

Mrs Mandy did the register. She said, 'We have a new boy today.'

She asked him a question, 'Are you afraid?' James screamed.

Mrs Mandy said, 'Don't be scared. This is Daniel. He's going to look after you.'

They all said
some sums.
James thought
they were hard.

It was playtime.
They all went
outside. James
didn't have anyone
to play with.

James wrote a story.
It was about people
with lots of friends.

At dinner time,
James was in the
orchard. He was
bored.

The Daniel said
'Do you want to
play with me?'

They played
'It'.

Then the bell went.
They went back
into the classroom.

James sat next
to Daniel.

When his
mum picked
him up he told
her all about
his first day.

James was happy.
He had a friend.

Summary

The number of children with autistic spectrum disorders in schools is many more than it was thought as recently as since 2002. Every school will have a number of children who have significant difficulties of an autistic nature, and many more children who will show some features of autism even if they do not fulfil all the criteria for a diagnosis. The school environment poses many challenges to these children, the nature of which may change over time. The move from primary to secondary school is often the most difficult and needs careful planning and management.

What is of most concern to the majority of autistic young people is having friends and being accepted by other children in their class. Vivid accounts by Louise, Brendan and Jordao illustrate how devastating bullying can be, and how powerless they have felt when teachers ignore their suffering. The bullying and difficulties they describe are unfortunately experienced by most autistic children in mainstream schools, and can affect these individuals long into adulthood. However, we have also seen the positive effects of targeted help at school through Owen's story, Martin's experience and the major effects of a teacher's intervention to help Connor through his anxiety on his first day. This illustrates that by small adaptations and thoughtfulness the lives of autistic children can be vastly improved at school, leaving them to enjoy learning and discovering. While their time at school may never be 'the best days of their lives', it is possible for everyone to work towards making them better.

Chapter 4

Me, My Friends and My Family

'My little brother' by Sam Lawrence's sister Elizabeth, aged 7

He giggles,
> sings,
>> reads lying upside down,
>>> talks to himself.

My little brother
> thinks he's a tiger.
He has hair like a hedgehog.
> He thinks he's a hero.
We call him piglet.
> He's always happy
>> ...until Mum says:
>>> 'No computer!'

Then he's
CROSS AS A WASP.
HE CROSSES HIS ARMS. HE STAMPS HIS FEET.
HE SHOUTS.
I tickle him.
> He giggles again.
>> ...I love my little brother

Finding out your child has autism is a difficult process for almost every family. To some parents it comes as a surprise, to others it's the end of a long, seemingly endless process of doctors, psychologists and assessments. What becomes clear from talking to families who have an autistic child is the variability in how they cope with the diagnosis, and then continue to go on functioning as a family. To some, the diagnosis feels unjust in some way, and there is a large period of adjustment, which may involve seeking a second opinion, or initially refusing to accept a professional's appraisal of their child. Others feel a huge sense of grief, needing to mourn the loss of a child they thought they had, and learn to accept a 'different' child. There are also parents, and indeed children themselves as we have seen in Chapter 2, who feel relief at there finally being an explanation for their behaviour and the way they think.

The role of the family in raising a child with autism is just as important as it is when raising a typically developing child. Views about this role have undergone significant change over the decades. In the 1940s, autism was seen to be caused by inadequate and emotionally absent parenting leading to the 'refrigerator mother' hypothesis. This damaging way of explaining a neurodevelopmental disorder resulted in a whole generation of families left confused and criticised about having an autistic child, and it doesn't take much imagination to predict the effect of this view on family life. Nowadays, science understands much more about the causes of autism, and this is likely to have an effect on the way children are viewed by their families, how children view their parents and importantly, how society as a whole views autism. There are now a large number of support groups for children, parents and siblings affected by autism, which aim to foster understanding and aid in coping with the condition within the family.

Does having an autistic child in the family change family relationships?

Relationships between an autistic child and their parents

Assessments for autism always include a detailed history of a child's development from birth. Most parents report that they noticed something was 'different' about their child from very early on – a difference that is magnified if they have had other typically developing children first. Differences reported include a child who cries more than unusual, is difficult to comfort and may not seek a lot of physical affection. Poor eye contact is also often noticed very early on in autistic infants.

As a child grows into a toddler, these differences in social interaction become more apparent and can often lead to parents feeling rejected, or that they are doing something terribly wrong in bringing up their child. This is all too often compounded by criticism from other family members, nursery school teachers or friends. One parent described how she and her daughter were in a supermarket when her daughter suddenly threw herself down on the floor and started to scream. Passers-by made comments about how her child was 'spoilt', 'naughty', 'out of control' and 'embarrassing'. Trying to explain that she was autistic was impossible and the family stopped going to supermarkets with their daughter from that day onwards.

There has been increasing interest in examining attachment between autistic children and their parents, although the number of scientific studies on this subject is still quite small. Attachment is conceptualised as 'the affectional bond or tie that infants form between themselves and their mother figure' (Bowlby 1982 [1969]). Early reports of children with autism by Kanner in 1943 include vivid descriptions of their 'indifference' to their parents. In the 1960s some theorists suggested autism might be primarily a disorder of the parent-child relationship (Mahler 1968). Recently, a review of this research (Rutgers *et al.* 2004) aimed to analyse all these studies to see whether there is something different about autistic children's attachment to their parents compared to typically developing children. As with all research, each study used a different group of children, and different methodologies (see Chapter 2). Using a statistical technique, the outcomes of all the studies on autism and attachment were considered. Rutgers *et al.* (2004) concluded that there was *no difference* in attachment security between typically developing children and high-functioning autistic children (i.e. those with normal IQ). Those with lower mental development showed more signs of insecurity in their attachments.

This finding certainly echoes the majority of parents who report that they do have a secure relationship with their autistic child, even though it may not be of exactly the same nature as the ones they have with their other children. Indeed, differences between a child with autism and their typically developing siblings are understandable due to the deficits autistic children have in emotional understanding and responsiveness, coupled with a reduced insight into social situations. Certain aspects of their behaviour, such as rigidity or aggression, also have an impact on close family relationships, but the often propagated view that all autistic children treat people like objects and do not form close relationships is not the case for most high-functioning children.

The insightful poem at the beginning of this chapter is written by Elizabeth Lawrence. Elizabeth's brother, Sam, has autism. Sam is also an exceptional artist, and often paints in the styles of famous artists such as Picasso and Van Gogh. Sam also paints pictures of his family – see the collection of portraits seen from his unique perspective. Martin Hal-fead also writes about the people in his family.

'My Family Gallery' by Sam Lawrence, aged 6

Self-portrait
This is a picture of myself. I did it when I was five years old. Mum watched me paint it from the other side of the table (so it was upside down), and only thought it was good when she turned it round!

My Mum

Sketch of Mum (after Picasso)

This picture is in the style of Picasso. I painted it after looking at Picasso's 'Woman Weeping'. In this picture Mum is not weeping but is smiling and feeling happy. I like the ears best because they look like Pokeballs!

My Uncle Stewart

This is a picture of my uncle, Stewart. What I like best about this picture is his glasses.

My Dad

This is a picture of my dad, Michael. This time it is in a combined style. First of all I did the painting with a big brush. Then, when it was dry, I added the features like his bristles with a black pen. This looks like my dad because he has sad eyes and a happy, smiley mouth.

My Granny

This is a picture of my Granny, Patricia. I drew this for her birthday. I think she looks delighted.

'My Family' by Martin Hal-fead, aged 14

My family is made up of my mum and my two sisters. My mum is originally from Holland, and is a very calm and thoughtful person with a great personality. My two sisters are twins who are both 11 years old but they are not identical. Louise is kind and quiet, both in her personality and the way she presents herself. Sylvia is almost her exact opposite, as she is loud and puts less thought into everything. They are all very understanding of me in their totally different ways.

Relationships between an autistic child and their siblings

There is a paucity of research concerning autistic children's relationships with their siblings. This is unfortunate because siblings provide an important context for social development (Dunn 1988). Travis and Sigman (1998) stress the importance of relationships with siblings as they 'may represent an intermediate level of social challenge between the highly supportive conditions provided by parents and the less supportive conditions encountered with peers' (p.70). They also bring to attention the high motivation of siblings to interact with an autistic brother or sister, and it has been found that autistic children spend a large percentage of their time with their siblings, which has important implications for their social development. For example, high-functioning autistic children can learn social behaviour and model what they do on the behaviour of a brother or sister. If they watch how a sibling makes two dolls talk to each other and interact, they can follow the lead and begin to understand in a more explicit way the social 'rules' which govern an interaction, such as saying 'hello' and 'goodbye', and how to ask conversational questions.

In addition to examining how sibling relationships develop between an autistic child and their brothers or sisters, it is also important to examine how siblings relate to their autistic sibling/s. There is often concern that siblings of autistic children feel they receive less attention and time than their autistic brother or sister and that all the interventions, social activities and groups for autistic children leave them out. Some research has indicated that siblings of autistic children are at risk of internalising and externalising adjustment problems (e.g. Gold 1993). Gold found higher levels of depression in siblings of boys with autism, and Bagenholm and Gillberg (1991) found higher levels of attention and conduct problems. However, as is usually the case, other studies have found very different results: that siblings are well adjusted, have positive self-concepts and healthy academic and behavioural adjustment (Mates 1990). Mixed findings have also been found regarding the social competence and peer relationships of siblings of children with autism.

One of the most recent studies by Kaminsky and Dewey (2002) aimed to investigate psycho-social adjustment in siblings of autistic children by comparing them to siblings of children with Down Syndrome and typically developing siblings. They found that siblings of autistic children were not at an increased risk of adjustment difficulties or loneliness and had high levels of social competence. Interestingly, there were a number of positive factors present in the sample of children they used for their study, which they suggest influenced this high level of adjustment. First, the majority of families were actively involved in support groups, so that siblings could interact with other siblings who had autistic brothers and sisters. This regular social support may facilitate healthy psychological adjustment. Second, better psychosocial adjustment was found in siblings when there were a larger number of siblings in the family. It is probable that having another typically developing sibling provides social support and is a 'buffer' for stressful experiences.

Writing on sibling relationships

The following piece of writing by James Woodcock is a valuable insight into his relationship with his siblings, in particular his sister, Heather. James highlights how important this relationship is in his life, and how his sister is his closest companion and confidante.

'The Angel of Light' by James Woodcock, aged 12

On the 29th April 2002, my little sister Heather was born. I awoke into her world a day later and walked into my dining room. Then I saw her, a little bundle wrapped in a soft blanket, in my mum's arms. I could have sworn that the clouds outside parted, for the sun to come out. My mum opened the blanket, so I might see my new baby sister.

Heather instantly struck me as beautiful. Her little thumb placed carefully in her mouth as she silently sucked it. Her lips were like roses in winter and her hair, though there was little of it, felt like silk. Unfortunately for her, her hair was blonde and this made her look like she had a yellow head. I held her in my arms, and she smiled at me with her delicate lips. I kissed her on the cheek, and the skin I felt was like glass, but with warmth and lovingness. The sun came through the open curtain and went straight into my sister's eyes. Her not used to the light, I moved her away from it and into my chest. I just hoped that this did not affect her sweet dream.

As my sister continued to grow, I noticed her love of water. As I watched her in her little tub (not a proper bath tub, with the risk of drowning, as she was still quite small). I watched her splash about. She was making awkward body movements, as if she was being kicked. Her face was red with exhaustion from all the splashing. The only awkward thing about her baths was that they were at funny times, like 10 o'clock in the morning and 3 o'clock in the afternoon, so usually I never except at weekends, got to see her in this enchanted state.

When I thought nothing could go wrong, it did, for Heather kept on vomiting her food and she was admitted to hospital. This worried me a lot as Heather was still quite young. When she came out of hospital three days later, she was diagnosed with gastric reflux. The doctors prescribed her two medicines that had to be taken daily. That day was not a happy one: the sky was grey, and it was raining.

Six months later Heather had not gained weight and was still vomiting. She had to have a machine in her stomach that would relay information to the hospital. This happened, but the hospital lost the results. Luckily the operation was not repeated as the doctors found she was allergic to milk.

Unlike any of my brothers, I felt I could tell Heather all my thoughts. I admired her for her calmness in a situation, and I often used to have a

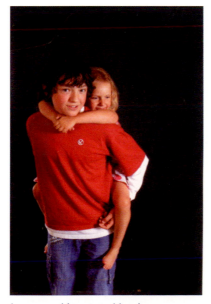

James and his sister Heather

conversation with her that no one else knew about. I never knew why. Was it because she couldn't tell anyone or because I trusted her? I think it was that I trusted her. Three and a half years went, and I still do. I also built up a lot of trust with her, unlike my brothers. This trust has continued throughout my relationship with her, and I respect her more than anyone else in my family.

My sister is a great sister and very bubbly. She is never dull; she always talks nonsense to the cashiers at the supermarket, who just smile at her. My sister is brighter than an angel, and that is what I will compare her to. Heather the angel of light is the best sister ever.

Friendships

'He had a birthday party last year, but we haven't had one since. No one came.'

Mother of autistic child aged 7

'He doesn't really have friends…he shows a strong preference for adults.'

Mother of autistic child aged 10

'Everything changed for me when I finally made a friend.'

Autistic teenager aged 13

Maria sits in the interview room swinging her legs. The toys have been put to one side and the psychologist is asking her questions. They talk about holidays, favourite things and pets. The assessment feels comfortable for her until she is asked about friendships. Maria names a few girls she knows at school but doesn't volunteer any more information about them. The psychologist wants to learn whether Maria understands what a friend is. She asks her how a friend might be different from someone she 'just knows' in her class. Maria stops kicking her legs and an expression of confusion comes over her face. She thinks for a few moments and replies rather matter-of-factly, 'Friends are different because they have different haircuts.'

'Friendship' is a concept which has no unified accepted definition, although most researchers perceive it as a 'close affective tie between children that is based on reciprocal and stable (six months and above) social interactions with a peer' (Buhrmester 1990). Friendships are important for developing prosocial behaviours such as sharing, giving and caring for another person, and also rely on a number of abilities such as the capacity to understand and consider the perspective of another individual, regulate emotion and develop strategies for conflict resolution (Asher,

Parker and Walker 1996). Difficulties in making friends and keeping friends are one of the hallmarks of social communication disorders. In every assessment for autism there are questions about friendship and, when speaking to autistic individuals of every age, managing friendships is an issue that never seems to go away.

Despite the many difficulties with friendships autistic children experience, it is a common misconception that they do not want to make friends, and are 'quite happy on their own'. This misconception is likely to have originated from Kanner's early clinical observations that autistic children have a 'basic desire for aloneness' (Kanner 1943). While this might be true for a small minority, most autistic children are desperate to make friends but don't know how to do so. Indeed, many report intense feelings of loneliness, and in a study by Bauminger and Kassari (2000) these feelings of loneliness are more intense and frequent than in typically developing children. However, interestingly, they also found that the constructs of friendship and loneliness are not linked in quite the same way as in typically developing children, so that an increase in friendships may not decrease feelings of loneliness. Bauminger and Kassari (2000) suggest that autistic children may lack the 'affective glue' to bind these two concepts together. If this is the case, they may benefit more from interventions that increase social knowledge and understanding, rather than those which try to motivate social involvement (Hurley-Geffner 1996).

As we have learnt from the children's writings about their experiences at school in Chapter 2, social knowledge and understanding are essential to establishing a friendship, which involves the capacity to understand a number of complex social rules and negotiations. While these may come naturally to typically developing children, they are a minefield to children with autism. Even into adulthood, many individuals report that, if only someone had told them exactly what to do when they met someone, they may have been able to establish a friendship, but that they couldn't think how to approach it on their own.

Early attempts to initiate contact with other children can result in the opposite to what an autistic child intended: 'He would initialise an interaction with a child in nursery by pushing them or hitting them' (parent of autistic child aged 3). As in the case of this child, other children become wary and stop approaching them to play. Teachers also perceive an aggressive child and may become punitive or keep the child away from the rest of the class. As a result, an autistic child may see any attempt to make contact with others as a failure, which may lead to withdrawal and/or low self-esteem. In later childhood, the social skills needed to become more complex: children need to understand the notion of friendship groups, sharing common interests with other children and reciprocity in a relationship.

Due to the complex nature of initiating and maintaining friendships, many autistic children rely heavily on their parents to help negotiate the relationships. Although children with autism and their mothers report that they do have friends (Bauminger and Kasari, 2000), research by Bauminger, Shulman and Agam (2003) suggests that these friendships 'very rarely emerge spontaneously or persevere without the help and mediation of others in the child's close social environment'. There were other noticeable differences in the *nature* of friendships. In comparison to typically developing children, those with autism had less stable friendships, met their friends less often and preferred more structured activities with friends, that required a lower level of social engagement, such as board games with clearly defined rules.

Friendships in young adulthood

As a teenager and young adult, there is a complex mixture of outcomes with respect to friendships. For some, the situation becomes harder as they lose the support of their parents and close social network. For example, John coped well while at school, with support from his mother when he had friends visiting the house, and in forming social contacts at a local youth group. However, when he went away to college, he found it difficult to approach other people and found himself staying in his room on his own. He became depressed at the lack of contact with others and eventually changed colleges to somewhere nearer his parents. This allowed him to live at home and continue to be supported with his social skills and his studies.

For other young people, there is no change in the nature of their friendships as they grow older, which leaves some autistic individuals feeling isolated and 'cut off' from the rest of the social world. Older teenagers report that they can feel rejected and 'left behind' by their peer group as their companions mature and begin to develop romantic relationships, and that the sense of difference from their peers becomes even more noticeable. Dating is another social situation that has a complex set of unwritten rules, and there is little in the way of intervention to help with this aspect of social development for autistic young people.

Although many young people still experience difficulties, others find that when they begin to specialise at college or in a job they are suddenly surrounded by people who enjoy the same things as them, and friendships are more easy to develop in this environment. For example, an overriding interest in science fiction may not win many friends at secondary school, but it would be ideal for a job in a specialist bookshop, which is likely to employ other enthusiasts. Many individuals also find that when they reach university there is such a large variety of people that they can find a group like them more easily by joining a society or club. For example, Sarah had few friends at secondary school and was treated as an outsider by her peers. She was dreading starting university as she feared that the bullying and exclusion from others would continue. However, when she arrived, she found a society that shared her interest in astronomy. Being among like-minded people, she found herself accepted into a friendship group and, although socialising was not easy, having a small group of friends she could rely on made a huge difference to her enjoyment at being away from home.

Children's perspectives on friendship

Friendship is discussed in some of the children's contributions about school in Chapter 3. The following short pieces of writing by Jordao, Holly and Martin focus on what it's like to make friends, what type of people are attractive as friends and what a friend actually is.

'Making Friends' from 'About me' by Jordao Allen, aged 15

It's not hard or easy to make friends. My friends think I'm the most annoying in the school but I'm still a good friend. Louis, Kieran, Shane, Michael, Lee, David and George will always be my good friends. I don't have a girlfriend but soon my time will finally arrive and who knows, maybe when I'm 18 it might be a teaching assistant who will always be at school except for Fridays...if I'm lucky...

'Making friends' Holly Maby, aged 11

I've just started secondary school. I find it hard to make friends so I haven't got anyone yet. I like talkative people so I don't have to be the one who is talking and it always happens that people are saying hello first. Smiley people get on my nerves.

'Friendships' by Martin Hal-fead, aged 14

I do find it hard to make friends sometimes, but this is largely due to the fact that I am quite picky about who I regard as a true friend. I think my mates know I have a very calm personality and that I am very loyal and thoughtful of their feelings and individual takes on life. I hang out with my friends Tim, Rory and Grant at school. I think a good friend is someone you can trust and who listens to your opinions. I think it is harder as you get older to make friends because as you get older your freedom is increased and weak people will turn away from those who have different thoughts about life.

Summary

Over the last few decades, there has been a dramatic change in thinking about the role of the family and of friendship in autism. The notion that autistic children are socially aloof with little need for friends or family is not the case for the majority. However, the desire to have relationships is often hindered by real difficulties in establishing, understanding and maintaining them. Children benefit from developing a 'toolkit' of skills that they can learn and apply in social situations, and from structured opportunities to interact with peers.

There are many ways to help autistic children establish friendships, such as encouraging them to join special social skills groups or structured organisations like the Scouts or church clubs and supporting them when friends come to play. Special interests and focused interest groups can also act as a 'gateway' to friendships. They offer a common interest to 'scaffold' social interaction and reduce situations that are particularly difficult for those with autism such as needing to make 'small talk'.

As the contributions in this chapter from the children demonstrate, just because navigating social relationships is more difficult it does not mean it is less important. In the childhood years, family can play an essential role in encouraging autistic children to form relationships without losing motivation or confidence if their first efforts are not successful, and in helping those around them to understand how mutually rewarding these relationships can be.

Chapter 5

Those Things that I Do – Obsessions and Special Interests

My obsessions used to be my protectors, but now they have taken me prisoner.

Mason Cooley (b.1927), aphorist

She is very sensitive to sound. I can't use the hair dryer or Hoover in the house. She also dislikes new clothes. I have to buy her the same clothes in bigger and bigger sizes.

Mother of autistic girl aged 5

He hates change. We had to buy a caravan so when we went on holiday it was 'home from home'.

Parent of autistic child aged 12

If I didn't stop her, she would watch TV all day with her face right up to the screen. If I turned it off she would scream until it is switched on again.

Parent of autistic child aged 4

Sensitivity to loud noises or unusual sounds or textures, insistence on sameness, need for routine, special interests, obsessions, list making, observing objects from unusual angles, lining things up in rows – the third aspect of the 'triad of impairment' – is the most poorly defined part of autism, and certainly not unique to it. Many other conditions such as Obsessive Compulsive Disorder (OCD) and Prader Willi Syndrome share features in common like routines, obsessions and insistence on sameness (Greaves *et al.* 2006). In addition, many of these behaviours can be found in typically developing children (Evans *et al.* 1997) tending to peak in this group from two to four years. These findings raise a number of important questions. First, what causes this collection of behaviours and is there anything different about them in autistic children compared to other clinical groups, or indeed typically developing children? Second, are they found in every young person with autism and what are the implications if they are not? Third, do they serve some beneficial function in addition to being classed as an impairment? Science does not know the answers to all these questions yet, but studies are being done to try and understand them better.

There have been many behavioural and neurophysiological explanations as to why children with autism engage in repetitive behaviours, have special interests or demonstrate particular sensory sensitivities (collectively referred to as 'scale D' behaviours). Kanner, who first described autism in 1943, described many 'autistic behaviours', including scale D behaviours, as being driven by anxiety. This view has been supported by a large body of research such as Howlin (1998), who found that stereotypical behaviours such as echolalia (repeating what other people say), flicking and hand flapping can all increase when an autistic child is anxious, as can more complex behaviour such as repetitive questioning. Thomas *et al.* (1998) propose that children engage in these behaviours to calm themselves down, and that the behaviours may serve the function of 'stress reduction'. Other theories put forward that scale D behaviours function as a means of escape, means of sensory reinforcement or as a means to modulate high levels of arousal.

Scale D behaviours are wider in scope than those behaviours that only contain a high sensory element. Because of the range of behaviours the term covers, it is highly improbable that one theory will account for them all, and some researchers have split the types of behaviours into different domains. A commonly used distinction is between 'lower order' and 'higher order' behaviours. Lower order behaviours include stereotyped movements, sensory interests and so on; higher order behaviours include obsessive interests, need for 'sameness' and rigid ways of thinking and behaving, and are seen as 'cognitively advanced' scale D behaviours (Turner 1999).

One of the most influential perspectives on the causes of obsessive behaviour has been that of an 'executive dysfunction' (Russell 1997). 'Executive functions' are functions in the brain which control behaviours by inhibiting actions, focusing attention selectively, planning and organising events and being able to shift from one perspective or way of thinking to another (such as being able to apply a new set of rules to the same game). Some people with autism have been found to have difficulties in these sorts of tasks, particularly in those measuring cognitive flexibility and inhibition. Cognitive flexibility has been linked specifically to rigid thinking and the need for sameness. In many ways this seems to make sense, because being obsessive about a particular subject or object shows some difficulty in moving onto a new topic of interest. However, problems in executive function are not exclusive to autism. They are also found in head-injured individuals who have damage to the frontal lobes in their brain, schizophrenics, people with OCD and those with ADHD. Most of the people in these groups, apart from those with OCD, do not develop obsessions; therefore we cannot assume that 'executive dysfunction' is solely responsible.

Other theories have examined scale D behaviours from the perspective of chemical imbalances in the brain such as abnormal levels of serotonin. In OCD, a common cause of treatment is to prescribe Selective Serotonin Reuptake Inhibitors (SSRIs), which have been shown to reduce obsessive and compulsive behaviour. A trial reported by McDougle, Kresch and Posey (2004) found that these drugs also helped reduce the same phenomena in autism. Are the behaviours in OCD and autism therefore the same? And can an individual with autism also have OCD as an additional diagnosis? Russell *et al.* (2005) compared a group of individuals with autism and OCD and found that they had similar frequencies of obsessive compulsive symptoms, but that the symptoms were more severe and interfered more with everyday life in individuals with OCD. The links between OCD and autism, and the boundaries placed on each diagnosis are not yet clear in science. However, increasing evidence from genetic studies suggests that there is a strong relationship between obsessive compulsive phenomenology and autistic symptoms (Hollander *et al.* 2003). Moreover, due to the overlap in brain regions which have also been found often to function differently in OCD and autism, there has been a move towards an autistic-obsessive compulsive syndrome (Gross-Isseroff, Hermesh and Weizman 2001). It remains to be seen what progress in classification, but also in the understanding of the mechanisms responsible for these behaviours, will develop in the future.

What is it like to experience both OCD and autism? The following extract describes the impact this has on Jake's life.

Extract from 'About me' by Jake Ballard, aged 17

Now I will talk a bit about how I am affected by Obsessive Compulsive Disorder. I JUST HAVE TO DO THINGS I JUST HAVE TO DO THINGS REALLY HAVE TO DO THINGS!!!!!!!!!!!!!!!!!!!! (17!s because I am 17). Some obsessions have been with me for as long as I remember but others come and go. When the short piece of film comes on before Eastenders or other BBC programmes (Indian dancing, wheel chair basketball players, tango dancers etc) I HAVE TO imitate their actions. Even if this annoys or embarrasses other people. If I don't do it I feel really agitated. I HAVE TO keep lists of everything I eat, what time I go to bed, every Citroen Picasso I see, statistics from my brother's football matches, what time I last boiled the kettle, and how long it took to boil, records from my football computer games. I do have other lists, but these are just the main ones.

Pot Noodles – a recent obsession for Jake

I am very obsessive about Pot Noodles at the moment. When we are out I FEEL I have to go and get the ones that I need. I go through the different flavours in my own order and eat them on a Monday and Friday for my lunch. If I am able to get the flavour I need in king size I have the king size on a Friday for a treat. I talk about Pot Noodles a lot and my mum says this obsession drives her nuts.

In the kitchen I like things done in a certain way. If my mum is making food for me, she HAS to get the plate and the cutlery from the cupboard and NOT off the draining board or I will not be able to eat it. I have to make sure that the tea and coffee and sugar containers are in a straight line on the surface. If they are not, it cheeses me off and I have to correct them. Also the mugs have to be on the stand in the right order. I am very jumpy when my mum puts things in the cupboards because I always think she is going to break something (I collect mugs and I have drinks in them in order and these are very precious to me). I had to make the difficult decision to stop buying them because there is no room left in the cupboards. I feel the need to time lots of things and my mum says that I am always looking at my watch. My major obsession at the moment is traffic lights. I LOVE THEM. I time them. My favourite light is the amber light when it is about to turn red because if you go through as it changes you feel like you have just made it. This feeling is excellent and it makes me feel YESSSS!, we went through an amber light! I talk about traffic lights a lot but my mum has explained that most people don't find them as interesting as I do.

ONLY JUST!

Other young people with autism who do not have OCD may also have obsessions that can become a large part of their everyday life. *Thomas the Tank Engine* is perhaps the most common obsessive interest in younger children reported by parents. As children get older, the nature of these obsessions or special interests often change as their general interests develop. Particular computer games, films or collectable cards often play a more prominent role for older children, and there are some interesting gender differences in the nature of obsessions. Clinicians report anecdotally that the nature of obsessions for girls can be of a more social nature, such as becoming particularly fixated with another person such as a classmate or a teacher. Other more female-specific obsessions reported by doctors and psychologists are fascinations with different types of breed of animal, television series such as *Friends* and 'fantasy worlds'.

Holly describes the nature of her special interests and obsessions, which highlights their varying nature but also some of the complex issues which can arise from them:

'The trouble with obsessions' by Holly Sidaway, aged 18

I have periodic obsessions. I think of them as being like periods in natural history, Palaeozoic, Mesozoic, etc. The subject of these obsessions can be anything. Pets, fictional characters, or even types of car. They are quite intense, and can last any length of time from a week to over a year, almost completely taking over my mind for this period. This caused a problem recently, as I became obsessed with a friend I had made over the Internet. He found my intense interest in him quite disturbing, and refused to communicate with me for a long time. Eventually, the situation was resolved, and I find I am no longer obsessed with him, although we still talk occasionally. From this experience, I have learnt to be more careful in dealing with people.

Meeting people on the Internet is popular with autistic teenagers

I met the man (Mark) in an Internet forum where people discuss the computer game Half-life (my major obsession before I met Mark). From our mutual interest in Half-life, we developed a close friendship over a time of a few months. But the trouble was, he was my only friend. I became too demanding of attention from him, as I had nobody else to talk to. This was okay at first, as Mark seemed to like me very much, and we had many long chats. But when he began to have less time for me, I became quite upset.

It was then that he realised that I had an unhealthily intense interest in him, and he began to refuse all contact with me. I found this very hard to deal with, and the next few months were a waking nightmare.

With some help from my father, I eventually managed to re-establish contact with Mark. After all that had happened, I realised that I needed to be more careful. I tried to be less demanding, aware that I could easily scare Mark away again. I liked to imagine that he was a nervous, wild animal that I was attempting to coax closer to me.

I further cemented our relationship on his birthday, by sending him some clay model animals I had made. He was pleased with them, and thanked me, telling me that I had 'made his day'.

In the following month, I found myself losing interest in Mark. I had been obsessed with him for just over a year, and it was time for me to change. I went back to some of my older obsessions, including the aforementioned computer game.

We are still not as close as we once were, and I am less interested in him than I used to be. But I am still happy that he is there, if I need him.

He was my greatest obsession, and my first true friend.

Special interests in earlier childhood

We have seen from the insightful writing from Jake and Holly how obsessions and special interests can affect teenagers. How might they play a part in younger autistic children's lives? In this section, George, Zak, Joseph, Brendan, Patrick and Beau illustrate this for themselves.

On the next page is an illustration of the *Thunderbirds*, which George's mother describes as being a 'passion of his'.

At times, special interests can come into the classroom and into other subjects. The following illustration by Zak is an example of how this happened at school. Zak had a very special interest in the London Underground. He knew all the stations and the routes between them. At school, Zak was in a religious studies lesson, learning about Jesus at the temple in Jerusalem. The teacher asked the class to draw a picture to illustrate the story, and here is what Zak drew:

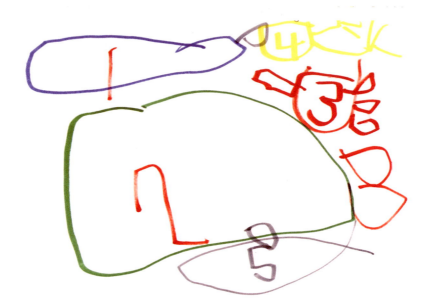

'Thunderbirds are go!' by George Fiddes, aged 6

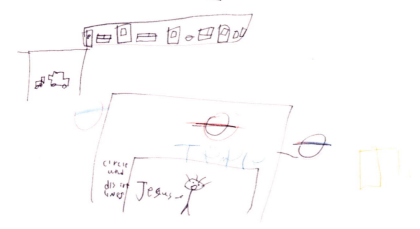

'Jesus at the temple' by Zak Ellis, aged 7
'Circle and District Line, Jesus'

Special interests in the form of transport, particularly trains, are very common in the early years. The following is a piece of writing by Beau about how much transport means to him, instigated by a task at school to 'Describe a type of vehicle.'

'I love....' by Beau Newman, aged 10

I love buses. I love fire vehicles. I love trains. I love cars and I love taxis. I love vans. I love trucks and I love Royal Mail vans. I love planes and I love helicopters. I love engines. I love balloons. I love birds. I love police cars. I love games. I love peoples and I love it! I love rockets. I love coaches and I love boats. I love racers. I love vehicles. I love THAMESLINK trains. I love Southern trains and I love Virgin trains and I love GNER trains. I love London buses. I love London taxis. I love the London Underground. I love the Blue Bell Railway and I love railways.

The next contribution is from Joseph who is older and has a special interest and passion for music and film.

'Media' by Joseph Cleaver, aged 12

I like a lot of things such as swimming, film and music – but let's move on to those last 2 things.

You see if you were to ask me what is my favourite film it would be like what is the meaning of life! I have many favourites from JASON AND THE ARGONAUGHTS to EDWARD SCISSORHANDS, from gangster spoof BUGSY MALONE to crime comedy THE LADYKILLERS (ALEC GUINNESS).

And as for music I love a big range from bluegrass to big band, from bebop to a little bit of rock, I don't like all rock but some songs from the old bands such as The Who and The Clash. I like world music beats all from Guinean all-stars Bembeya jazz to west Saharan Tuareg blues band Tinariwen (Mali is the country); from African rappers (Senegal), Positive Black Soul to the peaceful alpine-Italian vocals of Cantovivo's Alberto Cesa (pronounced chesa).

I also like playing the drums and I'm teaching myself the piano.

As mentioned in the previous section, particular television programmes or characters often become a favourite special interest for children with autism. The following drawings from Brendan illustrate his particular obsession with

SpongeBob and movies he has seen. His mother explains that Brendan is obsessed with videos, especially cartoons. Recently he has been told he cannot watch cartoons at school any longer, which 'has been very stressful for him. He will do anything to access a cartoon!'

'SpongeBob' by Brendan O'Leary, aged 9

'Making movies' by Brendan O'Leary, aged 9

Special interests are sometimes more unusual than films or music, and may concern things that may not be of interest to many people, such as plastic bottles, milk tops and drain pipes. A distinction can be drawn here between circumscribed interests and unusual preoccupations. Circumscribed interests are things that may be of interest to typically developing children, but for an autistic child they do not have a strong social element (such as playing with another child who has an interest in trains). Unusual preoccupations are interests in things that would not usually be of interest to others, as in the case of Patrick. Patrick has had a fascination with street lamps and road junctions since he was young, which have lasted for a number of years. Here are two photographs of Patrick's special interests. The first is a model he made with bricks of motorway junctions. The second shows him on the beach, using sticks to recreate street lamps on an imaginary highway:

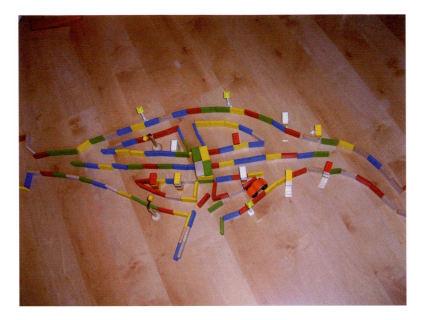

'Motorway Junction' by Patrick Harper, aged 9

'Highway on the beach' by Patrick Harper, aged 9

Patrick has had a number of other special interests over the years, and has a precise memory of when they occurred. Here he lists interests old and new:

'My interests' by Patrick Harper, aged 9

WHAT I USED TO BE INTERESTED IN:

Recording (7-9 years), playing my keyboard (2-9 years), playing with lego (Building roads with lego, 3+), drawing maps (6-8 years), drawing mazes (7-9 years), composing songs (7-8.5 years).

WHAT I'M INTERESTED IN NOW:

Playing on the computer/laptop (8+ years), playing on the PlayStation (7.5+ years), street lamps (3+ years), piano (6+ years), singing (7+ years), earthquakes (8+ years).

Lessons from obsessions – how they can be used positively in everyday life

> It seems that for success in science or art a dash of autism is essential. For success the necessary ingredients may be an ability to turn away from the everyday world, from the simple practical, an ability to rethink a subject with originality so as to create in new trodden ways, with all abilities canalised into one speciality. (Hans Asperger)

As we have learnt from the children who have contributed their experiences in this chapter, obsessions span an extensive range of subjects, objects and activities. Some can last for a few months and others for years, taking up varying amounts of time and effort. Although they can be extremely impairing, many people today and throughout history have used their ability to focus on a small range or one particular thing to become very successful individuals.

Ioan James (2003) wrote an article on 'Singular scientists' in which he examined the lives of people such as Isaac Newton and Albert Einstein who retrospectively are thought to have had something very similar to Asperger Syndrome. It is interesting that they viewed social contacts as something that distracted them from important work, and both had a history of being isolated and lonely as children. How did their obsessions contribute to such famous achievements? James (2003) remarks that it is the *nature* of their obsessions – namely, with scientific problems which had yet to be solved – which led to their singularity and determi-nation to provide solutions. Einstein was certainly clear about the genesis of his dis-coveries: 'I know quite certainly that I myself have no special talent; curiosity, obsession and dogged endurance, combined with self-criticism have brought me to my ideas.'

'Albert Einstein' by Sam Lawrence, aged 8

Many children with autism have interests in new technologies such as computer programming and gaming, where their specialist knowledge and intense interest could forseeably lead to new discoveries and advances in a rapidly growing and competitive field. The patience and commitment needed to test new software, for example, may be ideally suited to a style of thinking and pattern of working seen in autistic individuals who can work for days, perhaps even months, on the same topic without boredom and often approach problems from a 'different angle' to find a novel solution.

Even brilliant individuals, however, had obsessions which were likely to have hindered as well as helped them, and this side to creative genius is often overlooked in a desire to 'over-romanticise' such personal histories. Newton, although producing excellent science, also had a fascination with alchemy which had little scientific merit. He also had compulsions, such as the need to copy by hand large bodies of text repeatedly, text that was often wholly unrelated to his work. There are countless other famous individuals in history who suffered from compulsions and obsessions. Now that we have an understanding of these behaviours, we realise that these geniuses were in fact suffering from disorders and, had they been living today, would have been given a diagnosis. It's a fascinating question how history might have changed if they had received help with these often crippling behaviours, but it also raises interesting questions concerning how we view these behaviours today. There is certainly a need to evaluate interventions for affected individuals and the types of obsessions that are targeted by treatments. However, if an intervention aims to 'extinguish' all obsessive behaviour, there could be a danger of not only extinguishing obsessions that do no harm, but also those which might be of benefit.

Using obsessions and special interests more widely

Not every obsession will be the beginning of an invention, career or hobby. While many autistic children adore *Thomas the Tank Engine* when they are young, it is unlikely that the majority will go on to be train drivers. However, many parents are keen that something 'useful' should be gained from the large number of hours dedicated to *Thomas* every day. There are many ways in which obsessions can be used to help children with everyday tasks, whether in school or at home.

Creating tools to help children use special interests

On a recent visit to a primary school, a teaching assistant had been working with a young boy with autism who had a special interest in *The Simpsons*. Instead of banning this in the classroom, she had made cut-out characters with speech bubbles, which had key instructions and reassurances. For example, if a certain situation was anxiety-provoking, she would direct the boy's attention to Homer Simpson whose speech bubble said 'You have someone to help you, there's no need to worry'. These statements were found to be far more effective if they were 'spoken' by a favourite character than by a teacher. Other ideas at home and school include daily and weekly timetables with tracks, which *Thomas the Tank Engine* chugs along to show what the child is doing now and what is 'further on down the track'. Key facts to learn, rules and social skills can also be taught incorporating a special interest. Children are often keen to contribute to these schemes and to be part of brainstorming ideas that work for them.

Using special interests as rewards and incentives

'I don't want to go to the party, I want to play on the computer!' 'I want to draw Power Rangers not maths diagrams!' A special interest will always seem a more appealing alternative to tasks an autistic child does not want to do. How might a teacher or parent use them to encourage engagement with unpopular activities? In much the same way, all children enjoy being rewarded for behaviour, perhaps by using a star chart or points scheme; autistic children can be rewarded by time for their special interest. This could be a direct exchange – one hour of sitting with the family at dinner is 'exchanged' for one hour on the Playstation. It may also be a system of points, so that five mornings in which the child is ready on time to leave for school could earn five stars towards a comic or DVD of their favourite television series.

These are just two suggested ways to incorporate special interests into everyday activities. There are hundreds of ideas exchanged in books, support groups and on the internet. Many books and articles are dedicated to this area and have proven a great resource for parents and teachers.

Does everyone with autism have this collection of behaviours and interests?

In Chapter 1, the criteria for a diagnosis of autism were outlined. The key features were summarised as a 'triad of impairment', and a child needs to have clinically significant difficulties in each domain to be given a diagnosis of autism. The third element of this triad encompasses a range of stereotyped and repetitive behaviours, special interests, sensory sensitivities and interests, resistance to change and fondness of routines, among others. However, many children on the autistic spectrum do not show significant impairment in this domain (Tanguay, Robertson and Derrick 1998). It has also been established that these behaviours may not all cluster together consistently in children with autism, and most children certainly do not show all of them.

Many hundreds of children referred to clinics with very poor social interaction and communication skills cannot receive a diagnosis of 'autism' because they do not have a substantial impairment in the third element of the triad. However, they are often just as impaired socially as children who do have all three elements and in some cases their social communication impairments may be more severe. It varies from clinic to clinic, but these children are typically labelled as having 'atypical autism' (ICD-10) or PDD-NOS (DSM-1V) These labels can be misleading. 'Atypical autism' suggests there is something unusual about the manifestation of social and communicative difficulties and it can be interpreted that they are not as severe as 'autism proper'. PDD is a term so ubiquitous that many parents and schools are confused about its ambiguity and implications for the child in question. Again, it is often assumed that a child with PDD is less severely affected than a child with autism. This may be true in some cases, but it is misleading to use PDD as a general 'mild kind of autism' label. Children who have a diagnosis of Asperger Syndrome are also viewed as more mildly affected, when in reality they are often as severely affected as an 'autistic' child, but have an Asperger diagnosis because they had no language delay. Part of this confusion lies in the variability of terminology used by psychiatrists, paediatricians and psychologists. Terms used also vary from clinic to clinic and some clinicians are not consistent in their own day-to-day practice with the criteria system they employ.

Future directions

Scientific research in the field in some areas is moving towards a re-conceptualisation of autism, based on bi-dimensional structure – that is, one based on (1) social communication and (2) reciprocal social interaction impairments. In twin studies, it has been found that there is a significant aggregation of symptoms for social reciprocity, and language and imagination impairments, but not for repetitive behaviours (Spiker *et al.* 2002). Reasons for this change in the conceptualisation of autism are likely to be, in part, due to changes in how some researchers think about autism's relationship to typical development. The notion that autistic disorders differ qualitatively from typical development has been challenged by population studies (Tanguay *et al.* 1998), although a large body of science still treats it as if it were a categorically separate condition. Owing to the amount of overlap autistic symptomatology has with other disorders, it is also difficult, particularly when studying obsessions, stereotyped behaviours and special interests, to assess what, if any, of these behaviours are exclusive to autism.

Summary

Although not seen in all children with social communication disorders, behaviours that fall under the third element of the 'triad of impairment' can play a large role in an autistic child's life and that of their family. We have seen how Jake's life is dictated by his obsessions and routines, and the impact that has on daily activities. Holly illustrates strikingly how obsessions with people emerge, and how the advent of new technologies such as internet chat rooms can be a positive forum for developing social interaction skills but one that also needs to be approached with caution.

George, Zak, Brendan, Beau, Patrick and Joseph show a variety of special interests – some that have been transient and others that have lasted throughout their early childhoods. These interests can be used to engage children, enhance learning and make the environment more familiar and reassuring both at home and at school. Their potential for incentives and rewards also ensures even obsessions that seem 'pointless' can be used positively.

Research into these behaviours is gaining international attention as they are so varied yet so central to our current diagnostic classification systems. However, research is still in its infancy. Some particular behaviours in this domain have been linked to specific biological systems, and a closer examination of these mechanisms, coupled with more detailed and systematic measurement of related behaviours, holds much promise for future understanding and the development of treatments.

Chapter 6

The Future

'Adam's world' by Adam Smalley, aged 9

Before I knew I had social communication disorders
I daydreamed all day.
Now I play with my gang
Because my mum helped me make my gang.
I like having friends more than daydreaming
I like having friends lots and daydreaming is boring.

I like science because I think it's interesting
I hate R.E. because I don't believe in god
I don't like most subjects that involve writing.
When I grow up I want to get married
And have children
I also want to design engines.

One of the most common questions asked in clinics assessing children for autism is 'What's the prognosis for the future?' It is an important question, but one of the most difficult to answer. This often results in an unsatisfactory 'wait and see' approach or a general 'it's different for every child so it's impossible to say'. This chapter attempts to give an overview of some of the research that has been conducted looking specifically at outcomes for children with autism. A number of children and young people have also shared their hopes and plans for the future, and there is work from a young artist at the start of his professional career.

Navigating outcome research – making sense of the studies

In Chapter 1 there is a section on becoming a discerning reader of autism research (p.13). Among other issues, it outlines how essential it is to check that the research you are reading is about children who are similar to your child. This is a particularly important point when it comes to reading outcome studies because the outcomes for individuals with autism are hugely variable. This is due to:

- most studies employing very small numbers of children (sample sizes)

- children being selected in inconsistent ways across studies so that in some cases an official diagnosis may never have been made, and in others only severely affected individuals may have given consent to participation

- differences in socioeconomic status, educational/psychosocial support and geographical location

- differences in tools such as questionnaires/assessments used to quantify outcome measures.

Across studies there are many other factors not listed here which affect outcome.

To date, there are very few studies that have looked at outcome for high-functioning individuals – most concern low-functioning children whose future independence and prospects are affected by moderate to severe learning disabilities. The paucity of research in this area is a result of poor identification of higher functioning individuals, who are only just beginning to be recognised and helped.

Perspectives on outcome: From Asperger to the present

Anecdotally, Hans Asperger predicted a positive outcome for his original patients who were more intellectually able – particularly those who could use their special talents or interests to gain employment or to integrate socially (Howlin and Goode 1998). He reported that many of his patients went on to become successful scientists, mathematicians and high-ranking civil servants.

It wasn't until much later that more systematic studies looked more formally at outcome. In general, it has been found that while diagnosis remains stable, outcome is more varied. The best predictors of a 'good' outcome (acceptable functioning in social, work or school arenas) are IQ (particularly verbal IQ above 70) and language development – specifically the presence of meaningful speech before six years (Lincoln *et al.* 1988, Lord and Bailey 2002). Despite this however, even individuals with high IQ have a variable outcome, which may depend on factors such as the degree of social support offered by the family, intervention and support from appropriate services, and employment status (Lord and Venter 1992).

Educational outcome

Chapter 3 discussed some of the issues regarding schooling, particularly the difficulties in transferring from primary school with consistent routines and staffing to secondary school with multiple teachers, classrooms and subjects. These transitions can be made less distressing for autistic individuals if carefully planned and executed. Even in the cases where young people do have a distressing experience at school, most students with autism complete secondary education with some assistance (Tsatsanis 2003). Assistance may be needed because, as Howlin *et al.* (2004) suggest, the fundamental deficits of autism may 'swamp' the effects of high intelligence. As we have seen in Chapter 3, it is certainly the case that many autistic individuals do not reach the potential predicted by their IQ, and need support to achieve this goal.

Conditions for individuals with social communication disorders have dramatically improved with regard to further education. Szatmari *et al.* (1989) found that half his sample went on to college or university and 44 per cent went on to obtain a university degree. In England, the Special Educational Needs and Disability Act 2001 (SENDA) has established legal rights for disabled students and has outlawed discrimination in education at all ages. This means autism can be declared on a university application form such as the UCAS form in the UK. There are mixed feelings from adolescents about declaring a social communication disorder to a university. Some feel they do not want it to be considered when they apply, or to be part of their personal profile. However, there are some advantages, such as being able to claim extra allowances to help with studies and being able to access extra support that universities have put in place. For more information, the Asperger's Syndrome Foundation (www.aspergerfoundation.org.uk) has produced an information sheet on going to university. The National Autistic Society also provides support in higher education through Prospects student support mainly in the London area, although they are now offering new one-off consultancy training courses more extensively across the country.

Employment

Applying for a job and succeeding within an organisation requires more than academic ability. It demands a degree of social skill and intuition to liaise with clients, complete interviews and understand the often tacit political issues in an office, at the same time as producing a high output of work. These skills, combined with the need to be able to handle stress, deadlines and manage people, are particularly difficult for individuals with autism. Adults often report difficulties when leaving the more protective environment of a university to enter employment because there is a general ignorance of autism in the workplace, which can lead to bullying and victimisation at work. Other adults find that they cope well in junior posts when they are managed closely and have a specified agenda to adhere to. However, if they are promoted and have to manage others, they often cannot cope and either resign or lose their jobs. Figures for rates of employment differ between studies, from almost all individuals being employed or in sheltered work schemes in Szatmari *et al.* (1989) to only 27 per cent in a study by Mawhood, Howlin and Rutter 2000. Again, as with general outcome, while there are many intervening factors that could explain why some individuals are more successful than others, there is a positive relationship between IQ and employment. Factors in the workplace such as supportive colleagues and management, and an appreciation of the many positive factors an autistic person can bring to a job, are also important. For example, an autistic individual is more likely to be honest, punctual, reliable and pay attention to detail. They are also less likely to be distracted by office gossip and keep focused on their work.

Mawhood and Howlin (1999) demonstrated that access to specialist employment schemes could significantly improve the chances of individuals finding and maintaining suitable employment. Prospects, an employment programme run by the National Autistic Society has branches throughout the UK and aims to help both employers and employees with the recruitment, training and retention of staff through the government's 'Access to Work' scheme. They provide a wide range of services such as the Prospects Transitions Project, which helps students in the London area with the transition from the final years of their degree to employment, and training for employers on how to manage autistic individuals. There are also a number of books on the market that specifically target employment and business issues.

Psychiatric issues

No-one can ignore the fact that services for children are many times more numerous than those for adults, and this can hit families particularly hard when a child transfers officially from child to adult services. This period of time has frequently been described by parents as the 'black hole'. It is compounded by the fact that, while the National Health Service in the UK has identified mental health and learning difficulties as priorities, high-functioning autistic individuals are left out of both. Psychiatric issues, however, can begin to play a more prominent role around this transition period (see Chapter 2. p.21 for more on psychiatric comorbidity). Tantam (2000) discusses how the desire for social interaction, coupled with the awareness of repeated failures in coping with the social world, can lead to depression as the social pressures increase with age. It is therefore essential that associated psychiatric issues are addressed and treated as this has been found to improve overall outcome by decreasing problematic behaviours in the adolescent and reducing disruption in the family. Indeed, helping the family to cope has been shown to improve the medical outcome of children; therefore, reducing family pressure in families affected by autism may help to mitigate behavioural or psychiatric issues in the affected individual (Tantam 2000).

Another issue regarding psychiatric symptoms becomes important when a young person with autism reaches adulthood – that they may be 're-diagnosed' with a different condition, such as psychosis or personality disorder. This is not the same as being diagnosed with an additional disorder, rather it is given *in place* of the original diagnosis. There are some symptoms which are similar between autism and psychosis (Berney 2004); however, treatment is not likely to be appropriate or effective if the diagnosis is confused, and may consist of powerful neuroleptic drugs. This is an area which needs more research and targeted training because many adult psychiatrists are not familiar with the presentation of social communication disorders in adulthood.

Social and interpersonal outcome

Social communication impairments are at the heart of autistic individuals' difficulties and, although some show improvements in social skills and friendships, most adults still report these areas as ones of extreme difficulty. Studies are varied in outcome with regard to personal relationships – in some a quarter of subjects had dated regularly and formed long-term relationships (Szatmari *et al.* 1989), in others (Mawhood *et al.* 2000) only one individual had a serious relationship with a member of the opposite sex. Figures for friendship were also variable, and it was noted that many needed the context and structure of a social club or organisation to maintain friendships over time.

With regard to living arrangements, many adults still live at home with their parents, or in supported accommodation, but there is still a paucity of research into this area and this may not reflect the current situation. What is clear, however, is there is a life-long discrepancy between cognitive ability and social adaptive function that is at the heart of autism (Tsatsanis 2003). As outcome continues to improve, and prospects continue to increase when compared to even a few years ago, it is hoped that these two aspects will be drawn closer together in the future.

Children's writing about the future

Reading outcome research in autism can sometimes paint a bleak long-term picture. There follows a selection of drawings and writings from autistic children about their hopes and dreams for the future. Contrary to popular belief, not all autistic children want to become engineers or computer programmers. There is a wide range of careers they wish to pursue, and for some they are making steps towards their future careers already. The following contributions by Louise and Martin describe their ambitions to become writers.

'The future' by Louise Parker, aged 12

My main ambition is to move from Southampton to Norfolk as soon as I can after leaving school. Both sides of my family live up there, and it's where my parents come from. People say that people with Asperger's are usually the last ones to leave home. They don't go until their twenties, apparently. I need to ignore that bit and concentrate on getting there.

I will achieve this by getting a Saturday job as soon as I am old enough and by writing books – hopefully. I know how tricky it is to get one published. A book may be flatly refused, or at least told that it can only be accepted if you tweak about with this bit here that's not quite right. At the moment I am writing one similar to this one, and I am doing a small comedy thing. I was also working on a fiction piece that will take a while to complete. I need something published if I am going to buy a flat or mobile home by eighteen.

Apart from being a successful author and moving to Norfolk, my ambitions include being a bit more hard-working – industrious, if you like. I have a bit of a mental block at the moment. I have no willpower to do anything. Everything's for later and that needs to change. I am also trying to learn the original Wingdings font – though God knows what I'll use that knowledge for!

I am considering fostering – though that isn't definite – to be perfectly honest nothing is, but I also have storylines and characters planned for years ahead. I am impatient with things and need to know what I'm doing. I tend to take possibilities into advance, work related or otherwise, years before they could come into practice. One book may be tricky. I need permission as the basic foundations came courtesy of a children's game show that aired 2003/2004. It may also be hard to get published as I have no idea where to end it or how to make it worth reading. But these characters I have are special. I know most of them inside out, back to front and will get them in a book somehow – no will not be accepted!

I am already planning on making things reality, and something I've got in mind now will happen in the future, even if it's just buying cat food in Tesco's – for a cat, that is, not for me!

'The future' by Martin Hal-fead, aged 14

In the future I would like to become a published author because I enjoy writing and I am very good at English. I would like to be a journalist when I grow up as I am interested in travelling and exploring in new places. I hope that one day I will win an award for literature and be recognised as a famous author.

Joseph wrote about his special interest in film and music in Chapter 5, p.77. Here he talks about his plans to direct films, learn foreign languages and have 'a place to call home'.

'Hopes and dreams for the future' by Joseph Cleaver, aged 12

My hopes and dreams for the future are to become a weight lifter or film director.

The films and serials I have in mind for the film directing career are westerns and spy serials.

I hope to win a gold medal in a weight lifting contest, I might not, but I like to test my strength.

I want to be bi-lingual and speak Arabic.

When I grow up I want a little place that I can call home. It will have a television with cable, one bedroom, a dining room and a kitchen, which will be painted white. Also I will have a garden and grow food.

Brendan also has plans for the future working in his favourite restaurant so he can 'get a lot of money' to put in the bank.

'When I grow up' by Brendan O'Leary, aged 9
'When I grow up I can get a job on a restaurant. I would be the cashier, get a lot of money, put it in the bank.'
  'Welcome to Clancey's restaurant. Can I take your order?'

Below, Jordao shares his passion for travel and how his plans for the future involve trying new food, speaking new languages and visiting new places. He also lists things he would like to see change in the world as part of his hopes and dreams.

'The Future' by Jordao Allen, aged 15

The most obvious things you'll see in the future are flying cars, robots, futuristic buildings and PlayStations 20s.

When I grow up I want to be in Japan, Tokyo, because even though understanding languages is obviously too complicated, I wanted to check out the famous Mt Fuji, become the first to play PS4, check out Japanese animation and delicious sushi and rice rolls. It's the best way to live, peacefully and quietly.

My second dream is USA because there are lots of lands to discover including Illinois, Philadelphia, Texas, Washington DC, N.Y. and all the other states. America is the 'world police' and they'll do whatever it takes to keep the order of the world. It's the home of our favourite movies, TV shows, sports and other stuff.

My hopes and dreams are: stop all killings, drugs, pirate DVDs and bullying.

Owen enjoys drawing and playing on the computer. He hopes to combine these two interests in the future by making computer games.

'When I grow up' by Owen Oakley Darwin, aged 10
'When I grow up I want to make PC games.'

Nathan has recently left school and is now at art college. He has sold seven paintings to date. Here are some of his paintings and statements that explain the ideas behind each work.

A selection of recent works by Nathan Cash Davidson, aged 18

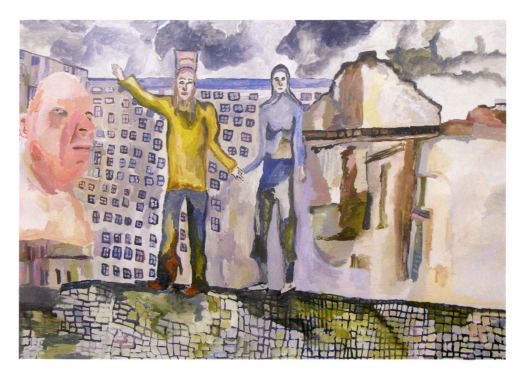

Golden monkey ridicule

I called the painting this title, because at first I wanted to use the title for my other painting. The other painting had an optical illusion head that looked like a monkey skull with a feathery hairstyle when turned upside down. I thought in my head, that when the head wobbled it was like a golden monkey skull with a feathery hairstyle, which I imagined in my head waving from side to side and I thought that would go well with 'ridicule'. But then I gave that title to the one without the optical head to the one with the normal head. This painting is about a couple that live in a block of flats, and they're waving to mid air to escape a picture on their flat wall of a wrestler's face. The wrestler is called 'Kane'.

Trellick Tower commission

This guy called Alex wanted me to do a commission for him. At first I was asking my dad how to sell paintings, but he told me it would be a tricky situation. Then we put a picture of my Trellick Tower picture from my GCSE piece up onto Ebay. Then Alex bought that copy for five pounds, and then he asked me to do a portrait of his block of flats (Trellick Tower), so I painted Trellick Tower with Flames coming out of the roof, and a picture of a green devil, but Alex's wife thought that was of her.

He caned his back to cause a war
The idea behind this is that a clown entertainer takes a wand out of his pocket while performing to a bunch of children. The wand extends and turns to a cane, which whacks him, round the back. This caused the Queen to eat 'punch' from the puppet show 'Punch and Judy' and that caused all the bodybuilders round the world to have a war with the chavs that started a world war.

Smirking cookies
This painting is about different heads on a building by 'Antoni Gaudí'. The different heads on there are a mannequin head, Jeremy Irons, my dad, and me with a girl from a film. Like I fight with paint at night I painted the background white.

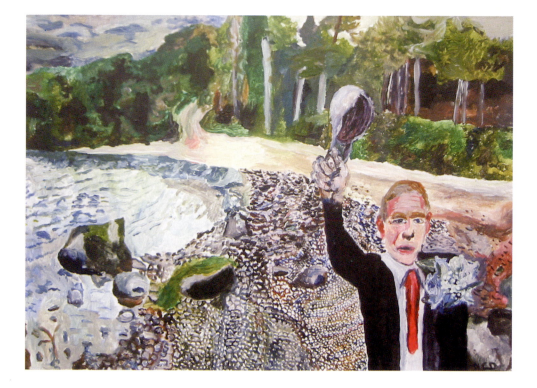

Bush lends his hat

There was a time to sniper a viper riper, learn from your rivals and fight the disciples, the tallest tower is hidden in the smallest flower like a linier razor on George Bush's blazer, carefully done when I could have had fun, he was meant to lend his hat to whoever he was looking at whereas my idea was hidden inner-ear, which some people fear, I cease to delete this as a went to pick up the pieces, the situations do hide fine then comply it to mine, to make my day his image that faded away like a blur so don't stir the cat's fur but first rehearse the lines in this verse, a glorified gleemy glide is snitchfully seemingly fly but hard labour is a fat man's whack flavour.

Lend to the king's dungeon

I'm waiting to say that this painting is about the growl of two cats, one rapper and snap, bang woo tang oh lack dagger fang. The rapper on the snapper in his impatience in the station is Snoop Dog, what an ovation. He is crossing the boarder by playing the recorder and near his lap are his two cats.

Summary

The future is never certain for anyone. Those who have autism have many things written by others about how their lives will develop over time, yet there is no consensus on what this path of development will be, particularly in high-functioning individuals.

What is clear is that early intervention and acknowledgment can help improve outcome by improving social skills and also reducing the effects and occurrence of associated difficulties such as psychiatric disorders. Appropriate support through education and employment can increase confidence and self-esteem, which are also important factors for developing as an adult.

Ambitions and hopes for children with autism are changing. Once seen as a disability resulting in life-long isolation and dependence, the children in this book have shown there is another story to be told, and in the future a new chapter will unfold.

References

American Psychiatric Association (1994) *Diagnostic And Statistical Manual Of Mental Disorders* (4th edn) (DSM-IV) Washington, DC: American Psychiatric Association.

Asher, S.R., Parker, J.G. and Walker, D.L. (1996) 'Distinguishing friendship from acceptance: Implications for intervention and assessment.' In W.M. Bukowski, A.F. Newcomb and W.W. Hartup (eds) *The Company They Keep: Friendships in Childhood and Adolescence* (pp.266–405). Cambridge: Cambridge University Press.

Asperger, H. (1944) 'Die autischen psychopathen im Kindersalter.' *Arch psychiatrie Nervenkrankheiten 17*, 76–136.

Aynsley-Green, A. (2006) *From Punishment to Problem Solving: A New Approach to Children in Trouble.* London: The Centre for Crime and Justice Studies, King's College.

Bagenholm, A. and Gillberg, C. (1991) 'Psychosocial effects on siblings of children with autism and mental retardation: A population-based study.' *Journal of Mental Deficiency Research 35*, 4, 291–307.

Baird, G., Simonoff, E., Pickles, A., Chandler, S., Loucas, T., Meldrum, D. and Charman, T. (2006) 'Prevalence of disorders of the autism spectrum in a population cohort of children in South Thames: the Special Needs and Autism Project (SNAP). *Lancet 368*, 9531, 210–215.

Barnard, J., Prior, A. and Potter, D. (2000) *Inclusion and Autism: Is it Working?* London: The National Autistic Society.

Barnard, J., Potter, D., Broach, S. and Prior, A. (2001) *Autism in Schools: Crisis or Challenge?* London: The National Autistic Society.

Bauminger, N. and Kassari, C. (2000) 'Loneliness and friendship in high functioning children with autism.' *Child Development 71*, 447–456.

Bauminger, N., Shulman, C. and Agam, G. (2003) 'Peer interaction and loneliness in high-functioning children with autism.' *Journal of Autism and Developmental Disorders 33*, 5, 489–507.

Berney, T. (2004) 'Asperger Syndrome from childhood into adulthood.' *Advances in Psychiatric Treatment 10*, 341–351.

Bowlby, J. (1982 [1969]) 'Attachment and loss: Retrospect and prospect.' *American Journal of Orthopsychiatry 52*, 664–678.

Buhrmester, D. (1990) 'Intimacy of friendship, interpersonal competence and adjustment during preadolescence and adolescence.' *Child Development 61*, 1101–1111.

Dunn, J. (1988) 'Sibling influences on childhood development.' *Journal of Child Psychology and Psychiatry 29*, 119–127.

Evans, D.W., Leckman, J.F., Carter, A., Reznick, J.S., Henshaw, D., King, R.A. and Pauls, D. (1997) '"Ritual, habit and perfectionism" The prevalence and development of compulsive-like behaviour in normal young children.' *Child Development 68*, 1, 58–68.

Gadow, K.D., DeVincent, C., Pomeroy, J. and Azizian, A. (2005) 'Comparison of DSM-1V symptoms in elementary school-aged children with PDD versus clinic and community samples.' *Autism 9*, 392–415.

Ghaziuddin, M. (2006) *Mental Health Aspects of Autism and Asperger Syndrome.* London: Jessica Kingsley Publishers.

Ghaziuddin, M., Weidmer-Mikhail, E. and Ghaziuddin, N. (1998) 'Comorbidity of Asperger Syndrome: A preliminary report.' *Journal of Intellectual Disability Research 4*, 279–283.

Gilmour, J., Hill, B., Place, M. and Skuse, D.H. (2004) 'Social communication deficits in conduct disorder: A clinical and community survey.' *Journal of Child Psychology and Psychiatry 45*, 5, 967–978.

Gold, N. (1993) 'Depression and social adjustment in siblings of boys with autism.' *Journal of Autism and Developmental Disorders 23*, 147–163.

Grandin, T. (2001) *Teaching Tips for Children and Adults with Autism.* www.autism.org/temple/tips

Greaves, N., Prince, E., Evans, D.W. and Charman, T. (2006) 'Repetitive and ritualistic behaviour in children with Prader Willi Syndrome and children with autism.' *Journal of Intellectual Disabilities Research 50*, 2, 92–100.

Gross-Isseroff, R., Hermesh, H. and Weizman, A. (2001) 'Obsessive Compulsive behaviour in autism – towards an autistic-obsessive compulsive syndrome?' *World Journal of Biological Psychiatry 2*, 193–197.

Hollander, E., King, A., Delaney, K., Smith, C.J. and Silverman, J.M. (2003) 'Obsessive-compulsive behaviour in parents of multiplex families.' *Psychiatry Research 111*, 11–16.

Howlin, P. (1998) 'Practitioner review: Psychological and educational treatments for autism.' *Journal of Child Psychology and Psychiatry 39*, 3, 307–322.

Howlin, P. and Goode, S. (1998) 'Outcome in adult life for people with autism and Asperger's Syndrome.' In F.R. Volkmar (ed.) *Autism and Pervasive Developmental Disorders.* Cambridge: Cambridge University Press.

Howlin, P., Goode, S., Hutton, J. and Rutter, M. (2004) 'Adult outcome for children with autism.' *Journal of Child Psychology and Psychiatry 45*, 2, 212–229.

Hurley-Geffner, C.M. (1996) 'Friendship between children with and without developmental disabilities.' In R.L. Koegel and L.K. Koegel (eds) *Teaching Children with Autism. Strategies for Initiating Positive Interactions and Improving Learning Opportunities* (pp.105–127). Baltimore: Brook.

James, I. (2003) 'Singular scientists.' *Journal of the Royal Society of Medicine 96*, 36–39.

Kaminsky, L. and Dewey, D. (2002) 'Psychosocial adjustment in siblings of children with autism.' *Journal of Child Psychology and Psychiatry 43*, 2, 225–232.

Kanner, L. (1943) 'Autistic disturbances of affective contact.' *Nervous Child 2*, 217–250.

Kim, J., Szatmari, P., Bryson, S., Steiner, D. and Wilson, F. (2000) 'The prevalence of anxiety and mood problems among children with autism and Asperger Syndrome.' *Autism 4*, 2, 117–132.

Leyfer, O.T., Folstein, S.E., Bacalman, S., Davis, N.O., Dinh, E., Morgan, J., Tager-Flusberg, H. and Lainhart, J.E. (2006) 'Comorbid psychiatric disorders in children with autism: Interview development and rates of disorders.' *Journal of Autism and Developmental Disorders*, July 15.

Lincoln, A.J., Courchesne, E., Kilman, B.A., Elmasian, R. and Alen, M. (1988) 'A study of intellectual abilities in high functioning people with autism.' *Journal of Autism and Developmental Disorders 18*, 505–524.

Lord, C. and Bailey, A. (2002) 'Autism spectrum disorders.' In M. Rutter and E. Taylor (eds) *Child and Adolescent Psychiatry* (4th edn, pp.664–681). Oxford: Blackwell Scientific.

Lord, C. and Venter, A. (1992) 'Outcome and follow-up studies of high functioning autistic individuals.' In E. Schopler and G.B. Mesibov (eds) *High Functioning Individuals with Autism* (pp.187–200). New York: Plenum.

Mahler, M.S. (1968) *On Human Symbiosis and the Vicissitudes of Individuation: 1. Infant Psychosis.* New York: International Universities Press.

Mates, T.E. (1990) 'Siblings of autistic children: Their adjustment and performance at home and school.' *Journal of Autism and Developmental Disorders 20*, 545–553.

Mawhood, L.M. and Howlin, P. (1999) 'The outcome of a supported employment scheme for high functioning adults with autism or Asperger Syndrome.' *Autism: International Journal of Research and Practice 3*, 229–253.

Mawhood, L.M., Howlin, P. and Rutter, M. (2000) 'Autism and developmental receptive language disorder: A follow-up comparison in early adult life: 1. Cognitive and language outcomes.' *Journal of Child Psychology and Psychiatry 41*, 547–559.

McDougle, C.J., Kresch, L.E. and Posey, D.J. (2004) 'Repetitive thoughts and behavior in pervasive developmental disorders: Treatment with serotonin reuptake inhibitors.' *Journal of Autism and Developmental Disorders 30*, 5, 427–435.

Medical Research Council (2001) *MRC Review of Autism Research: Epidemiology and Causes.* London: Medical Research Council.

Moyes, R.A. (2001) *Incorporating Social Goals in The Classroom: A Guide for Teachers and Parents of Children with High-functioning Autism.* London: Jessica Kingsley Publishers.

Newton, C., Taylor, G. and Wilson, D. (1996) 'Circles of friends: An inclusive approach to meeting emotional and behavioural needs.' *Educational Psychology in Practice 11*, 4.

Russell, J. (1997) *Autism as an Executive Disorder.* Oxford: Oxford University Press.

Russell, A.J., Mataix-Cols, D., Anson, M. and Murphy, D.G.M. (2005) 'Obsessions and compulsions in Asperger Syndrome and high functioning autism.' *The British Journal of Psychiatry 186*, 525–528.

Rutgers, A.H., Bakermans-Kranenburg, M.J., van Ijzendoorn, M.H. and van Berckelaer-Onnes, I.A. (2004) 'Autism and attachment: a meta-analytic review.' *Journal of Child Psychology and Psychiatry 45*, 6, 1123–1134.

Spiker, D., Lotspeich, I., Dimiceli, S., Meres, R. and Risch, N. (2002) 'Behavioural phenotype variation in autism multiplex families: Evidence for a severity gradient.' *American Journal of Medical Genetics 114*, 129–136.

Szatmari, P., Bartolucci, G., Bremner, R.S., Bond, S. and Rich, S. (1989) 'A follow up study of high functioning autistic children.' *Journal of Autism and Developmental Disorders 19*, 213–226.

Tanguay, P.E., Roberston, J. and Derrick, A. (1998) 'A dimensional classification of autism spectrum disorder by social communication domains.' *Journal of American Academy of Child and Adolescent Psychiatry 37*, 271–277.

Tantam, D. (2000) 'Adolescence and adulthood of individuals with Asperger syndrome.' In A. Klin, F.R. Volkmar and S.S. Sparrow (eds) *Asperger Syndrome* (pp.367–399). New York: Guilford Press.

Taylor, G. (1997) 'Community building in schools: Developing a "circle of friends".' *Educational and Child Psychology 14*, 3.

Thomas, G., Barrat, P., Clewley, H., Joy, H., Potter, M. and Whitaker, P. (1998) *Asperger Syndrome: Practical Strategies for the Classroom.* London: The National Autistic Society.

Travis, L. and Sigman, M.L. (1998) 'Social deficits and interpersonal relationships in autism.' *Mental Retardation and Developmental Disabilities Reviews 4*, 65–72.

Tsatsanis K.D. (2003) 'Outcome research in Asperger Syndrome and Autism.' *Child and Adolescent Psychiatric Clinics of North America 12*, 47–63.

Turner, M. (1999) 'Repetitive behaviour in autism: A review of psychological research.' *Journal of Child Psychology and Psychiatry 40*, 6, 839–849.

Whitaker, P., Barratt, P., Joy, H., Potter, M. and Thomas, G. (1998) 'Children with autism and peer group support: Using "circle of friends".' *British Journal of Special Education 25*, 2, 60–64.

White, A. (2004) 'What are the effects of cognitively behavioural therapy in children with autistic spectrum disorders?' The Wessex Institute for Health Research and Development Succinct and Timely Evaluated Evidence Reviews, Vol 4.

Wing, L. (1981) 'Asperger's Syndrome: A clinical account.' *Psychological Medicine 11*, 115–119.

World Health Organisation (1992) *The ICD-10 International Classification of Mental and Behavioural Disorders.* Geneva: World Health Organisation.

Biographies

Jordao Allen, aged 15

Pages 19, 37, 67 and 95

My name is Jordao Allen and I go to Garratt Park School. I'm in year 10 and autistic. My class is 10RB. Some of the people in my class are really annoying but we'll still always be friends.

Jake Michael Lavous Ballard, aged 17

Pages 20, 22 and 72

My name is Jake Michael Lavous Ballard and I live in Farnbourough with my parents and my brother and sister. My sister is called Bianca and she is 15 and my brother is called Marlon and he is almost 13. I go to Osbourne College in Winchester and I have a best friend there called Craig. Craig likes to tape videos tapes and likes trying to get out of the classroom to look for them. I have a good relationship with my dad when we watch my brother play football together. I feel like one of the men. My Mum and I have a laugh with different catch phrases.

Ryan Boatright, aged 13

Page 28

I am 13. I go to Rydens School. I like riding my bike, going to the youth club, reading and gardening. I have a younger brother and sister. They do not have autism.

Nathan Cash Davidson, aged 18

Pages 26 and 97–102

Music influences my paintings as well as smell and memory. I play the guitar, and enjoy listening to a wide variety of music and I can make up my own raps. I regularly go to exhibitions, art galleries and museums. I am now at art college and I have sold 7 paintings.

Joseph Cleaver, aged 13

Pages 77 and 93

My name is Joe C. Cleaver (b.1994). I have to wear glasses because of my poor eyesight, but that doesn't bother me. I'm 12 years old and go to Langtree School on the border between Berkshire and Oxfordshire.

Zak Ellis, aged 11

Page 76

I live with my sister, three brothers, mum and dad. I am very into trains and love the London underground – I can draw the whole network map from memory. I love playing football, and am the goal keeper in our school team.

George Fiddes, aged 6

Page 76

Hello, my name is George. I am 6 years old. I like going swimming. I go to school and my favourite lesson is reading.

Martin Hal-fead, aged 14

Pages 29, 38, 61, 68 and 93

My name is Martin Hal-fead and I live in Leigh with my two sisters and my mum Ellie. I am 14 years old and go to St Thomas More High School. I like karate and football. My favourite subjects in school are English and Science.

Patrick Harper, aged 9

Pages 27, 80 and 81

My name is Patrick Harper. I like playing on the computer, recording on cassettes, swimming at Esporta, singing in church and playing the piano.

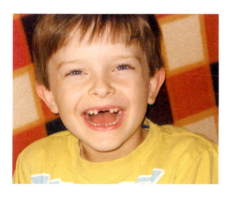

Sam Lawrence, aged 7

Pages 58–60 and 82

Sam is seven years old. He goes to school part time, and enjoys reading time and science best. When he grows up he wants to be a genetic engineer because he says it would help people if he could grow an extra liver. His interests are Bionicles, computer games, playing football with his dad and reading. He describes himself as 'clever, funny and kind'.

Holly Maby, aged 11

Page 67

My name is Holly and I live in Essex with my mum, dad and younger brother and sister. I have just started secondary school.

Beau Newman, aged 10

Page 77

My name is Beau. I am 10. I like going to school. I like break time because I like to play with my friends. My best friends are Frank, Matthew, Harry and Gus. I like to learn about space and trains. My brother Hamilton likes aeroplanes, airports and Lego. I like aeroplanes and airports too. I like steam trains, London North East Railway, London Mid South, British Rail, Great Western Railways and Southern Railways. I like making models out of paper. I like to eat Dairylea Dunkers.

Owen Oakley Darwin, aged 10

Pages 17, 24–25, 39–40 and 96

My name is Owen. I am 10 years old. I like to learn about the body and robots and space and aliens. I love the Simms. I live with my mum and dad and sisters Jem, 15, who has Asperger Syndrome, Camilla, 13, and Miranda, 8. We have 6 pets. My best friend's name is Henry. I like drawing.

Brendan O'Leary, aged 9

Pages 78–79 and 94

I'm special because I play Nintendo or watch real shows and cartoons. When I was in 3rd Grade Mrs Cousin said you can watch movies every day. I like going to the movies. I like to play with my brother, mom and me. I can't get a dog until Cameron goes to college. I'm going to be a teenager in 2009.

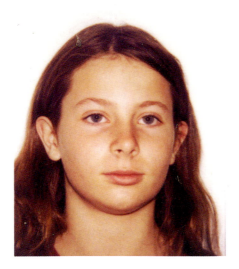

Louise Parker, aged 12

Pages 35, 41–42 and 92–3

My name is Louise. I am 12 years old and I live in Hampshire in the south of England. I would like to live in Norfolk as most of my family live there. I'm going to start looking for a place when I leave school. My school is called Wyvern Technology College and it's ok, but it's not the best place in the world. I am also writing a book about how secondary school is for people with Asperger Syndrome, and other high-functioning ASD people may also benefit. I am hoping it will be published but I'm not sure.

Holly Sidaway, aged 18

Page 74

My name is Holly Elizabeth O'Connor Sidaway. I have had a life-long interest in animals, especially parrots, and occasionally cats, dogs, cephalopods and lizards. I enjoy art, particularly drawing, and making and painting clay models. Sometimes I write short stories. And I read often. I especially enjoy works of fantasy and science fiction. My taste in film and television is similar to my taste in books. I am currently obsessed with the Half-life computer games, and several fictional characters that will remain unnamed. I am also becoming increasingly interested in the film Pirates of the Caribbean: Dead Man's Chest, having seen it several times already. One day I hope to have a job that will allow me to express my creativity. I would also like to travel around the world and help with the conservation of rare parrot species.

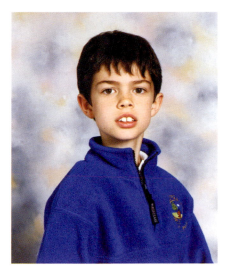

Adam Smalley, aged 9

Page 87

I've got a brother called Christian and a dog called Willow. I like engineering. I do things very slowly and it took me a long time to write 'Adam's world'.

Connor John Clancy Smith, aged 11

Pages 23 and 43–52

I am 9 years old. I do not have any brothers or sisters, just lots of cousins. I have two pet dogs. One is a German shepherd puppy that is 9 weeks old and the other is a whippet cross that is 13 years old. That's older than my mum in dog years. I live in south-east England, in Gillingham.

Janet Weedon-Skinner, aged 19

Page 18

Unlike my mum, I was born in England. I am now 19 years old. I have 3 brothers. I like to write short stories and poems. I have my own place now. I live only a few minutes away from my mum and dad. I also like to play on computer games. I like to watch films and read.

James Woodcock, aged 13

Page 62–64

I go to Westcliff High School for Boys, which is a grammar school. My hobbies include Warhammer which is a game where you buy miniatures, paint them and then play imaginary battles. I also enjoy cooking and I believe, although not everyone would agree, that my cooking is great. I have a secret ambition which is to give someone food poisoning!

Brendan Young, aged 16

Pages 29 and 36–37

I am an active teenager who very much enjoys the company of other active teenagers and enjoys having fun with playful animals along with other basics such as playing pool, snooker and video games, going to concerts with big time artists performing live, having fun in amusements/casinos, watching scary horror films and celebrity news and, to end it off, I am sadly disappointed about the 'hugely disproportionate' amount of discipline in Britain due to a/the lack of funds from our local government and council MPs to invest in fun teenage activities and to police who make Britain feel like a society and not scum-central.

Index